D1452340

SIMON CALLED PETER

DOM MAURO GIUSEPPE LEPORI

Simon
Called Peter

*In the Footsteps of
a Man Following God*

FOREWORD BY
ANGELO SCOLA

TRANSLATED BY
MATTHEW SHERRY

IGNATIUS PRESS   SAN FRANCISCO

Original Italian edition:
Simon Chiamato Pietro: Sui passi di un uomo alla sequela di Dio
© 2004 by Casa Editrice Marietti, S.p.A., Genoa and Milan

Ignatius Press is grateful to Sister Maria,
whose draft translation brought
this special book to our attention.

Cover art:
Icon of St. Peter. From Constantinople
(modern Istanbul, Turkey), around A.D. 1320.
British Museum, London, Great Britain.
© The Trustees of the British Museum/Art Resource, N.Y.

Cover design by Roxanne Mei Lum

© 2010 by Ignatius Press, San Francisco
All rights reserved
ISBN 978-1-58617-271-8
Library of Congress Control Number 2009934935
Printed in the United States of America ∞

To my community,
a gentle school
of the filial and fraternal
paternity of Christ

Contents

7

Foreword

I am grateful to Father Mauro Lepori, not only for what he has written in this book, but also for how he wrote it.

In fact, as I was reading it, I was again reminded of the wonders of the written page. The account takes you inside the events—in this case, the life of Simon Peter—and you see them with your own eyes; they penetrate your heart even more than if you had actually witnessed them.

Christian art has a special ability to do this, because it shares in the power of the Redeemer, who is closer to me than I am to myself, to penetrate the psyche.

So when, as in this case, the depiction of a saint emerges from a vigorous effort to get inside his human experience (the attempt to walk "in the footsteps of a man following God", as this book's subtitle says), it breaks through the limitations of mere "biography".

This book provides keen psychological insight into the life of the Prince of the Apostles, presenting an unmistakably human face in which we can all recognize some part of ourselves. So in addition to being an exquisite meditation, this book can also be read as a basic—but by no means dull—introduction to Christian anthropology.

Let's whet our appetite with a little sample.

In the first several pages, there is the description of how faith arises from an encounter that reveals man to himself: "Simon had never understood so clearly how important his life and freedom were." Or there is the insight into celibacy as the supreme exaltation of the natural capacity for affection: "So Simon left everything behind, in order that nothing might be lost."

For him, following Christ ("It was as if he had followed the Master where he was going, not only with his footsteps, but with his heart, his decisions, his teaching, his works") was the perfection of freedom and starkly highlighted the drama it entails: "He would never be able to reach the full depth of their friendship without embracing the Master's obscure destiny."

Peter had to face more and more clearly the fact that his integrity and salvation were to be found in his relationship with this Man: "Without him . . . he had nothing to think about except his own nothingness."

This meant achieving complete human maturity through the unbreakable bond between his Yes to Christ and his mission, in joyful obedience to the law of love: giving one's life for the work of Another. "They no longer had a moment for themselves: from sunrise to sunset, it was as if they were suspended between the mercy of Christ and human misery."

Simon Called Peter is an instance of a book being much more than just a book, as Guardini said: it is an encounter that adds another precious link to the chain of human friendship.

ANGELO CARDINAL SCOLA
Patriarch of Venice

Venice, April 25, 2004
Solemnity of Saint Mark
the Evangelist

Introduction

"And when they had brought their boats to land, they left everything and followed him" (Lk 5:11).

Is there anyone who is not moved by the witness of absolute dedication to Christ? This is the allure of the saints, whom the Church never tires of contemplating and of presenting as proof that it is possible to follow Jesus Christ with our entire selves, that it is possible to make a radical commitment to the Son of God, "the way, the truth, and the life" of man. The saints address our desire for the fullness of life and tell us that this is not an illusion, that it is not a mirage, but a call that resounds in the heart of every man and requires fulfillment. The answer to this desire is not a dream but rather the realism of following Christ. The realism of following Christ is demonstrated by the saints, those who followed him before us, leading us on toward him in an invisible chain stretching from the first steps of Mary and the apostles throughout all of history, until the Second Coming.

"They left everything and followed him." The allure of this radical response is lost unless we ourselves are moved by what we see in the saints and ask ourselves, "What does leaving everything to follow the Lord mean for us?" The saints teach us that the answer to this question is not the same for everyone. The saints teach us that "leaving everything" does not come before the act of following—instead, these two things happen at the same time. Leaving everything is done not only at the beginning but during the entire journey. Only death confirms, once and for all, our leaving everything behind in order to be with the Lord forever. Following him is a constant, renewed "leaving everything". It is never finished and continually requires a fresh commitment, as if each of the Lord's footsteps created another "everything" between himself and our freedom, a new "everything" to be left behind once again. This is how the love of Christ continues to live and grow.

The disciple and apostle Simon Peter is one of the most emblematic figures of the gripping drama of following Christ. He left everything right at the start, without hesitation, but he still had to confront the claims made on his freedom by Jesus, by circumstances, and by his own fragility and repeat his initial Yes to the very end. Peter's denial, but also the tradition of "Quo vadis?"—his last attempt to escape the total Yes of martyrdom by leaving Rome, and his encounter with Jesus, who asked him for a definitive "leaving everything" in dying for him—help us to understand that the freedom of total self-donation to Christ is a lifelong commitment. Because this commitment is asked of us by the Lord, it is always possible, in spite of everything, as for the repentant thief crucified next to Jesus.

At every stage of my journey as a man, a Christian, a monk, and an abbot, I have found Saint Peter as a companion walking ahead of me with my own humanity, with my own human poverty, full of contradictions. Peter is the saint in the Gospels who is most like us, the closest to our humanity, and yet also very close to Christ. We can always follow Peter. He always leads us to Jesus, he unites us to Jesus, because he never permitted his own fragility to separate his heart from Christ, even when he denied him.

And it is for this reason, I believe, that Simon Peter is the character we recognize best in the Gospels. We know all about Peter: his abilities and limitations, his sins and his sanctity, his psychology, his whole character. All of this lies before us absolutely clearly, so much so that at times he seems a bit superficial and crude to us.

Peter's transparency is gospel, is part of the gospel, of the good news of redemption in Christ. We can and must enter the school of Simon Peter, the school of his journey with Jesus, in order to follow the Lord as he wants to be followed, to cling to Christ as he enables us to love him.

I

"They cast their nets into the water"

(Matthew 4:18)

A fisherman casting his net—this is how the Son of God first saw Simon Peter, in his boat together with his brother Andrew.

Jesus was just walking by, as if by coincidence. He was a stranger as soon as he left the outskirts of Nazareth behind him. He did not have much to do yet, because the people did not know who he was, but this tranquillity would soon come to an end. For the time being, he was just strolling along the shore of the Sea of Galilee, looking at everything. Everything was beautiful for him, because in every detail of creation, in every nuance of the light and the weather, he saw the love of the Father, of his Father. Each gentle wave was like a ripple from a human heart overflowing with divine love at every pulse. Like the vast lake, glittering under the first light of dawn, he had only one desire: to spill out across that arid land teeming with creatures, with images of his own image.

But the waves roll in and roll out, and just a sprinkling of the immense power of the depths remains on dry land.

Jesus had seen the lake grow stormy many times since moving to Capernaum; he had seen it grow violent and lash against its shores. Men fled from it in terror. Only when the waves caressed the shores softly would they approach it and set out into it on their boats.

There he was, alone. How could his immense power, his divine omnipotence, be translated into a caress that would transform the world without compromising the freedom of love?

Right over there, there was a boat. His village was far from the lake, and he was fascinated every time he saw the immense expanse of water and men capable of confronting it. Now as well, he stopped to watch the two men in the boat. They looked like they were probably brothers. One of them—who must have been the older one—was calling out commands, while the other was quiet and reflective.

They were casting a trammel net, made with multiple walls of different widths of mesh that formed a sort of cage, making it difficult for the fish to find their way out.

The people in Nazareth lived by farming, growing grapes, and raising animals. It is very different to be a farmer or a shepherd as compared to a fisherman. The farmer sows the seed and prunes the vine. He knows that even if he doesn't see anything right away, the seed will sprout and bear fruit; he knows that the twisted stalk of the vine will produce leaves in the spring and fruit in the fall. The shepherd knows that the fertilized ewe will give birth at the proper time, and he sees the sheep's wool grow regularly. But the fisherman casts his net without ever being sure if he will catch anything. He can never make any predictions when he makes a cast. For the fisherman, the net expresses the uneasy anticipation of what the water will give, or not, according to its mood.

The fisherman does not cultivate the water the same way the farmer cultivates the soil. The fisherman does not care for his prey the way the sower cares for the seeds, then the sprouts, then the growing plants. The fisherman does not care for the fish the way the shepherd cares for the sheep. All the fisherman has to take care of is his boat and his nets. The rest is given to him.

Jesus saw fishermen often in Capernaum, on the shore mending their nets, torn here and there. There was no way for them to guarantee a large catch, but they could do their part. For them, the net was the faithful instrument of an anticipation without constraint or condition.

What a close resemblance it had to his own presence in the world, this casting of the net into the water, into the darkness of the water! How closely it resembled his Father's desire in sending him into the midst of an unpredictable, treacherous humanity!

Jesus smiled. He could not look at anything without relating it to his Father. The vinedresser made him think of the Father, who prunes human lives so that they may bear more fruit; the shepherd reminded him of the Father's tenderness; the sower reminded him of the Father's patience after sowing the Word.

But there was an intensity, an urgency, in the fisherman's casting out of his net that resembled more than any other human action the fire that the Father poured into his heart. Men must be saved! Men must be rescued from death and darkness!

Meanwhile, the two fishermen had pulled in their net. The catch was nothing special, and the older brother grumbled, seeming to criticize his younger brother, who listened patiently. The younger brother must have grown accustomed to his older brother's personality. Now the boat was coming ashore, and Jesus was so close to the lake that the cool foam from the waves was lapping at his dusty feet. He stared at the two men, and an immense flood of tenderness took hold of his heart. The two men noticed him, and Simon stopped complaining to his brother. "What in the world is he staring at us for?" he asked Andrew through clenched teeth. In silence, they continued with their cleanup routine, distracted by the man who seemed to be waiting for them on the shore.

Andrew whispered to Simon, "Now I recognize him: he's the rabbi I met the other day with John!"

But as they were getting off the boat, Simon saw that the man was looking at him more than at his brother. He had never seen such an appealing face, sad and joyful at the same time.

Simon felt an immense sweetness fill him. He forgot everything, all of his daily annoyances: the boat, the fish, the lake, his brother, his mother-in-law. Nothing else existed except for that face.

Suddenly, a faint sadness began to well up inside of him, as if from some hidden depth, a sadness he had never felt before. He was often in a bad mood, but it wasn't normal for him to be sad. And yet, somehow, that sadness seemed sweet to Simon. He had, as it were, drunk it from the eyes of that man, just as he had gulped down a jar of water that his wife had given him one day when he came home after fishing, sick of the lake water that had splashed all over him.

The man on the shore seemed lost in his own thoughts. He looked as though he had something to say. Simon was surprised to discover that he wanted to hear what it was, to draw it out of that strange, mysterious presence, like pulling the net back out of the water when it feels like there's something in it. It seemed that the sadness those eyes had imparted to him was heading somewhere, and the direction would be determined by what the man said. Simon intuited that his sadness left him no alternative between salvation and perdition. Without realizing it, his face was becoming serene, because he was forgetting the superficial tensions that had creased his forehead. What miracle was this, that was giving the irritable Simon the expression of a child? It was not until he felt a strange lump in his throat that he realized that this mysterious man was changing his heart. He smiled and knew that he had already accepted whatever words might come from the lips that were smiling back at him.

2

"But upon your word"

(Luke 5:5)

Simon and Andrew had worked the whole night without catching anything. They had thrown the net into the dark water again and again, with no success. Man is made to desire happiness, and it is hard for him to be unable to get what he wants.

They had already come ashore, together with the other fishermen. They were washing the nets—not only had their hopes been disappointed, but their equipment was fouled up with worthless junk. It would have been better to catch nothing at all, in total silence, rather than to have their hopes built up and let down that way.

And yet, if the fishing had been excellent, they would have had no time or opportunity to help the rabbi who was approaching them to ask if he could use their boat as a makeshift pulpit for his preaching. The crowd was crushing him. On the boat, a little away from the shore, he could speak and make himself heard more easily.

It is just when we are most exhausted and disappointed that Jesus comes to ask us to participate in his mission. Only afterward do we realize that our Yes was free in part because there was nothing to justify refusal.

As tired as he was, Simon probably did not catch much of Jesus' preaching to the crowd. But once again, it was good just to be near him. In his presence, although the weariness of that wasted night remained, the unhappiness was gone.

Jesus finally stopped speaking, which was not exactly a disappointment for the sleepy fishermen. A couple of oar strokes, and they would be getting back out to drag the boat onto the shore. One look from Jesus stopped them. It was the same expression Peter had seen the other day, and again he felt in his heart the desire for that word to which he would never say no.

"Put out into the deep and let down your nets for a catch" (Lk 5:4).

Simon hadn't been expecting this. He had been expecting a religious edict, something more spiritual, a message requiring long meditation. Why mess around with a man's fishing? This was exactly the kind of thing the rabbi could know nothing about. Besides, the idea made no sense at all. Go fishing in full daylight, when the whole night had been wasted? If anyone else had made such a suggestion, Simon would have really let him have it. But he couldn't talk that way to Jesus. So he limited himself to a simple observation: "Master, we toiled all night long and took nothing!" Almost against his will, he heard himself add, "But at your word I will let down the nets" (Lk 5:5). And to keep himself from thinking too much about how easily he had given in to the rabbi's unusual request, he immediately began rowing out to where he could cast the nets. His fishing companions followed, even less convinced than he was. But he had to admit that it felt good to row out into the deep water with Jesus in his boat, as if he had been given the gift of having him all to himself, far from the crowd still waiting for him on the shore to greet him, to touch him.

Jesus seemed so happy to get out onto the lake, with the sun already high above the glittering water. There was a radiance on his face like the happiness of childhood, before there is any anxiety to cloud a moment of pure joy.

Just as he was casting the nets, Simon couldn't help but think that this game the rabbi had gotten him into meant he would have to clean up again. But this sort of thought now tasted stale to something inside of him. He had no time to drive it away, though, because his halfhearted casting of the net was met by a hard tug that nearly pulled him into the water.

The men pulled back with all of their strength, and through the water they could already see that the nets were filled to the breaking point. It all happened so fast, so unexpectedly, that they did not even have time to wonder if they might be dreaming. Everything was so bizarre that a sense of terror overtook them—or maybe it was just the simple and real danger of seeing their boat capsize from the weight of the net. As if they were already shipwrecked, they began shouting to their friends on the other boat, who had been stunned to watch them row back out into the deep water for no apparent reason.

They could have simply let go of the net, dropping it into the lake. But the idea did not even enter their minds. There was a mysterious attraction binding them to that abundant catch. The strange thing was that this had nothing to do with greed for profit.

Everything happened fast, and yet each moment lasted for ages. It was all a blur of frantic movement, straining muscles, sweaty faces, splashing water, shouts, and grunting. Yet in the midst of all this confusion, there was only a single image burned into Simon's memory and awareness: the face of Jesus, who continued to smile at him, almost as if he were enjoying himself, even though the boat had become dangerous for him as well.

At one of the moments when the eyes of Simon and Jesus met, it was as if the poor fisherman were shouting to him, "Master, please, enough! We're going to die!" Were these words spoken, or were they only a thought? Finally they were able to divide the catch with the other boat and row back toward the shore, water sloshing around their feet, the fish still flopping around on the deck.

Simon's heart was racing from effort and emotion, and he gasped for breath as he made his way through the fish to where Jesus was sitting in the stern. Simon approached this man whose presence had become almost unbearable: they were too different, too distant, too "other". And yet it seemed to him that this presence was such an absolute gift to him that only Jesus could reestablish the correct distance between them.

Simon was overtaken by a sense of unworthiness: everything in his life that was petty, false, angry, silly, greedy, proud, vile had now become a heavy, nauseating heap.

He was surprised himself by what he cried out in front of everyone: "Depart from me, for I am a sinful man, O Lord" (Lk 5:8). And he knew that no truer words had ever come from his lips.

Even so, just as his words were disappearing into the noise of the water, the wind, the boat, Simon understood that these words, too, were false. They were no longer true before that face, before the expression of Jesus, who continued to stare at him in silence. The words were true inside of Peter himself, in his heart, in his humanity, but they were no longer true before Jesus. He had not yet finished saying, "Depart from me, Lord", when his heart began crying in desolation, "No! Stay with me, Lord! Take me with you!"

Simon was still on his knees in front of the Lord when the boat touched the sandy shore. Jesus stood up to get off the boat. He smiled at Simon and then looked off toward the clear horizon of the tranquil lake. "Do not be afraid; henceforth you will be catching men" (Lk 5:10). Simon understood that Jesus had already heard the cry of his heart.

3

"You shall be called Cephas"

(John 1:42)

What was Simon's first encounter with Jesus Christ?
Each Gospel gives a different version. What is certain
is that the Lord looked at him intently and called him.
In the Gospel according to John, Jesus is very direct:
Andrew "brought Simon to Jesus. Jesus looked at
him, and said, 'So you are Simon the son of John?
You shall be called Cephas' (which means Peter)"
(Jn 1:42).

What does it mean to have an encounter that changes
your life?

Simon must have guessed that if Jesus claimed the
right to call him by a new name, this meant that a
relationship with him was a call to become someone different from the man he had been in his own
eyes and in the eyes of others. The way that Jesus
looked at him was probably enough by itself to justify his mysterious right to destine Simon to become
someone other than who he thought he was. Jesus
demonstrated that he understood Andrew's brother
completely: "You are Simon the son of John." Jesus

was calling him specifically to become someone else
while still remaining himself.

In an instant, Simon realized that the entire distance
between who he was and this "Cephas, Peter" he
had to become was mysteriously bridged by the pro-
fundity of those eyes, so gentle and so terrible, that
were fixed on him. They were gentle because Simon
had never felt so understood, accepted, and forgiven.
They were terrible because Simon had never understood so clearly how important his life and freedom
were. Jesus was asking for everything he had, and it
would have been so easy to tell him no and slip away
from him forever. He didn't even have to say "yes"
or "no". He simply had to follow him, or let him go
and forget about him.

Forget him? Could he really have forgotten him?

And that name. What would Simon do with that
new name, Cephas? Would he use it like a surname?
But a surname almost always refers to something
amusing about a person, or an occupation, or his past
achievements. But for him, the name "Peter" would
instead recall the most dramatic moment of his life
and a task never finished, a mission never completed.

But in reality, what sort of task, what sort of mission,
was this?

Jesus gave him no explanation, no plan. The only perspective he had to offer was the gaze that he fixed on him, seeming to cast him out toward a boundless future in which his new name—Simon Peter—would find its full meaning and completion.

But did he really need any advance knowledge of this boundless future? Simon surprised himself by not giving it a single thought—he, who was usually so scrupulous in planning and preparing for every fishing expedition.

No, Simon was not thinking about the future. Was he thinking about his family, his home, his boat, his business? Yes, he thought about all of this, and in an instant he saw it all with complete clarity and in great detail. He had never before seen his life so clearly and how important everything in it was. He felt sad about his lack of attention and concern toward his family, his brother, his people, his work, his home, his boat, his nets, and himself. He realized that he was now looking at everything through the eyes of Jesus.

How could he abandon everything, now that it had become more important than ever before?

Simon felt that this new way of seeing things was drawing him close to everything and yet separating him from everything. Everything was suspended in the eyes of Jesus, and Simon was stunned when he realized that it was not only his own fate that was at stake but that of his family, Andrew, his home, his boat, and his hired hands. As in a whirlpool spinning faster and faster, he saw that even the fate of the lake, the mountains, the sky, the stars, the fish, the trees —everything, absolutely everything depended on his decision before the Lord. He was afraid, but to his astonishment, he saw that, as in the light of a lamp, even his fear had been accepted in the eyes of Jesus.

So Simon left everything behind, in order that nothing might be lost.

4

"Bid me come to you on the water"

(Matthew 14:28)

As they wandered around from place to place, Simon often thought back to the first words he had said to Jesus, before the miraculous catch: "But upon your word I will let down the nets." He had done nothing but respond simply to Jesus' request that he go out into the deep water and cast the nets. But since then, he had come to understand that every word he exchanged with Jesus had a life of its own, extending far beyond the circumstances in which it was pronounced. How many times, for example, when Peter had shown the negative side of his personality, when he had started grumbling about the other companions Jesus had chosen, or the uncomfortable life they were leading, or the suffocating, maddening crowd— how many times had he repeated to himself the urging of Jesus: "Put out into the deep." Simon loved this expression, he, the fisherman torn away from his occupation.

But it was not only the words of Jesus that lived on mysteriously in his mind; with time, his own words to Jesus took on a more profound meaning, like a wine that gets better with age.

"But upon your word . . ." Had Simon really come up with these words on his own? In any case, they were exactly right! In all the time he spent following Jesus, Peter often found himself completely baffled. But each time, he could repeat to himself and to Jesus: "But upon your word", I will continue; "upon your word", I will do this or that; "upon your word", I will try to accept and carry out what seems impossible to me. And when he did this, everything went better, for himself and for the others.

"But upon your word": even that "but" was well put, because each time, he had to accept a certain contradiction, to embrace something that he wouldn't have wanted to do if Jesus hadn't asked him or hadn't talked about it in his preaching to the disciples and the entire crowd.

"Upon your word". The words of the Master were truly something "upon" which he could lean, something "upon" which he could walk and move forward, like stones thrown into a swift current in order to enable him to leap safely across the danger.

Whenever he was having difficulty, Peter searched his memory of what Jesus had taught him for something that he could lean on, even if it had been something hard for him to take, something that had hurt him.

He was sure that one way or another, those words would help him to keep moving forward.

And if he could not remember anything to help him among the things Jesus had said in the past, he just went to him and asked him. Jesus always found the right words, he always went straight to the point, showing Peter everything in a new light. He was so happy to receive these treasures from the lips of the Master! He guarded them jealously, repeating them constantly, meditating on them ceaselessly, because they were sheer delight.

"But upon your word". Yes, it was true—even when Jesus' words were paradoxical, Peter could rely on them with his entire life, with everything in his heart.

That was how, one day, Simon tried to go beyond the possible in relying on the word of Jesus. It was just after the execution of John the Baptist. Jesus, as soon as he found out about this, surrounded as always by the noisy and demanding crowd, asked his disciples to get into their boat and go to a deserted place. He needed to be alone, naturally, because he loved John the Baptist, who was also his cousin. Peter and the others knew all of the peaceful spots on that immense lake. But it's hard to hide a boat in broad daylight, and the crowd was able to follow their movements from the shore, so when they landed they found the people already there.

Simon would have liked to have left again immediately, or to have driven away the crowd, telling them that the Master was in mourning and that they had to respect his sorrow. But Jesus, who was looking at the crowd from the boat, made an almost imperceptible gesture with his hand. "Let it go", he said, with a decisive tone that contrasted with the weakness of his voice.

It was always this way. He could be completely enveloped in prayer or dead tired, but as soon as he found himself before human misery, it hardly mattered whether it was a crowd or just one person. Jesus couldn't think of anything else. And that evening, he did not stop at a long instruction and healings. He multiplied five loaves and two fishes and was able to feed thousands of people.

At last he sent the crowd away, and this time he really did want to be alone. He even made the disciples leave in the boat, saying that he would catch up to them in Gennesaret the following day, even though he would be left without a boat of his own.

That makes no sense, Peter thought. But who dared to object to someone who performed those kinds of miracles?

To tell the truth, Simon had another reason to want to stay there with Jesus: the wind was not at all favorable, and that nighttime crossing was going to wear them out.

Once again, Simon said to himself, "But upon your word", stressing the "but" with a little anger, and set sail with the others. He watched Jesus walking away up the hill and into the distance, stooped over a bit from fatigue.

Nightfall came fast, and with it, the wind blowing against them picked up strength. Their boat was being tossed around like a piece of straw, and Simon figured that it was a good thing they had to row so hard, because otherwise they would have been complaining about Jesus for casting them off into this adventure without the slightest bit of good sense.

Of course, they could have spent the night where they had been, especially because they were stuffed with bread and fish. No one would have stopped Jesus from going off on his own to pray. Why put them into these extreme conditions, in which even their lives were in danger?

The first words Jesus had spoken to him one day had struck his mind like a bolt of lightning: "Put out into the deep and let down your nets" (Lk 5:4). But that had been during the daytime, Peter thought; the lake had been calm, and casting the nets hadn't been a problem. But now they had nothing to fish with, and even their oars were powerless against the fury of the waves.

A strange desperation seized his heart. He had left everything to follow the rabbi, because the extraordinary catch of fish on that first day promised marvels to those who believed in his words. Hadn't he been a little overhasty? Was it possible that he had sacrificed his life for a madman? John the Baptist, considered a great prophet by his brother Andrew and by Zebedee's son John, had already been eliminated. Why had he meddled with Herod's love affair? Everyone knows that kings are not saints. Not even David was. It is God who will judge the powerful. Jesus, too, was playing with fire. He was saying things that the people, sooner or later, would not tolerate.

Simon felt the anger rising up inside of him, but when it reached his throat it did not explode in insults and cursing as usual. Instead, it lodged there like a bitter lump. He felt an overwhelming desire to weep. In reality, he couldn't even tell whether he was already weeping or not, because everyone's expressions were masked by the crashing waves. But Peter knew that the distress on his own face wasn't from fear of the storm.

His head was so full of delirious thoughts of anguish and disappointment that at first he didn't wonder if the image appearing and disappearing amid the waves could be a living human being. Then the others began wailing and shouting, "Ghost! Ghost!" It was like the last straw for their strained spirits, exhausted by effort, danger, and fear. But then, on the edge of madness, came a voice, a warm voice, calm and familiar, speaking more to their hearts than to their ears, which had been deafened by the roaring of the waves.

"Take heart, it is I; have no fear" (Mt 14:27).

Peter felt that this voice was not talking to him about the fear of the storm and the wind but about the anguish into which he had plunged himself with his thoughts over the past few hours. The phantasm was not the presence walking on the water but the Jesus he had been imagining in the rage and desperate disappointment of that night. And in order to drive out that phantasm from his heart, he felt an immense need to talk to Jesus, to dialogue with him, because Jesus was truly real to him every time they talked together. He felt an intense need to touch him, to feel him near, a desire to go to him that was so strong that he didn't even think to wait until Jesus got into the boat.

But without really intending it, the words he heard himself saying had a challenging tone, and at that moment he realized that he had not yet completely forgiven Jesus for casting him into that night's abyss of madness and desperation.

"Lord, if it is you, bid me come to you on the water" (Mt 14:28).

Folly for folly. On the word of Jesus, he had agreed
to plunge blindly into senseless adventures, and walking on water was no less prudent than crossing the
lake in a full-blown storm on a flimsy fishing boat!

But Jesus' answer surprised him: "Come." For a
moment, Peter could see the Master's face, but he
couldn't tell whether his expression was one of fa-
therly compassion or an amused smile. To the amazement of his friends, Peter climbed over the side of the
boat. Before his feet even touched the water, he knew
that it was really Jesus out there waiting for him. Afterward he was never able to describe what it was like
to walk on water, and he needed the other disciples
to confirm for him that it really had happened. He
remembered a strange sensation of euphoria, a little
bit like the first time his father, John, had taken him
with him out onto the open water.

Jesus was not moving. Was he close? Was he far away?
It was impossible to tell. It was as if the distance
between him and the Lord varied according to the
thoughts and feelings in his heart. And just when
Simon started to feel proud of what he was doing,
a gust of wind blew in between him and Jesus, and
somehow in that moment he lost sight of the Master.
Far from the boat, without Jesus in view, he suddenly
found himself suspended above the restless lake. The
only thing he could do was sink. And in fact, he felt
himself plunge down, not only into the water, but

also into the dark thoughts and doubts that had tormented him all night long. His anguish was complete: he realized that he was sinking not out of weakness but out of pride and that death would not seal his powerlessness but his rebellion.

At that very moment, he saw Jesus looking at him. It was a look that forgave everything, and Peter reached out for it with a cry that seemed to come from his inmost depths: "Lord, save me!" (Mt 14:30).

At that same instant, a hand was grasping his own, firm and warm like a sunny shore.

5

"You are Peter"

(Matthew 16:18)

The months passed by. The disciples followed Jesus everywhere, but it was becoming increasingly difficult to understand where the rabbi was leading them. The enthusiasm of the crowds was not diminishing, but the hostility of their religious leaders was growing. For one thing, Jesus was doing nothing to win their favor. According to the Law, he spent time with impure people. His miracles violated the Sabbath, and this disturbed everyone—it was clear that he was doing good, but the Law is the Law, so which was more of God: the Law or the miracles?

Also, Jesus was very kind to everyone, including the Romans and the tax collectors, but he was very harsh with the Pharisees and Sadducees. This made ordinary people happy, because they had had enough of the Pharisees' and Sadducees' arrogance and greed, but everyone thought that the hostility between the rabbi and the big shots would not lead to anything good. The Pharisees and Sadducees were powerful and fanatical, while Jesus surrounded himself only with people of little social influence.

With time, the disciples realized that Jesus was also becoming more demanding of them. It wasn't that he was asking them to do anything difficult or burdensome—on the contrary, when it came to fasting, vigils, and observances, he was much less demanding than the Baptist or the Pharisees. Ultimately, Jesus demanded only one thing from them: that they trust in him. It was only when he realized that they didn't trust him that he got angry and became harsh toward them. Each time, they had to admit that they were truly ignorant, the way they forgot that they could trust him without reservation. But no matter how many times they reminded themselves of this, with every new situation, they inevitably fell into their usual reactions of fear, doubt, and worry. For instance, there had been the time they became anxious because they hadn't bought bread. Right after this, Jesus had multiplied the loaves and fishes a second time, feeding several thousand people.

They were sincerely saddened by their own lack of faith, because they could see that it hurt Jesus. Moreover, they often met poor people, even pagans, who demonstrated limitless trust in Jesus. Yet these people had not seen all of the miraculous signs that the disciples had witnessed up close, and they did not share the privilege of Jesus' constant presence and friendship. Jesus did not lose a single opportunity to praise the faith of these individuals, which made his saddened and embarrassed disciples think.

In other words, the more time went by, the more their following of Christ produced nothing but suffering because of their lack of faith, their inability to give Jesus the kind of trust that only he deserved.

One day, in the region of Caesarea Philippi, Jesus surprised them all with an unusual question: "Who do men say that I am?" (Mk 8:27). They replied that some thought he was the Baptist, or Elijah, or Jeremiah, or one of the other prophets. To tell the truth, this question made them uneasy—they really did care what the people thought about their Master, and they were afraid that Jesus was accusing them of depending too much on public opinion.

Jesus showed no reaction to the names that his embarrassed disciples listed for him. Then he was silent, so they thought that must be the end of the discussion. But suddenly the Master stopped, turned around, and looked at them. He had an ability to look at the whole group and each individual at the same time. "But who do you say that I am?" (Mk 8:29).

They all began to think, but the words froze in their throats when they looked into the gentle eyes of the Lord.

Their inability to answer this question seemed to leave them with no firm ground to stand on. How could this be? They had left everything for him, they had followed him for more than two years, they had endured every sort of discomfort for him—and still they couldn't say who Jesus Christ was for them! If only Jesus had given them the answer! If only the answer had come down from heaven! No, they couldn't put it into words. Jesus was a mystery, but they couldn't bring themselves to say that and nothing else.

So when Peter spoke, his voice was like the echo of a clap of thunder from a deep, cavernous abyss: "You are the Christ, the Son of the living God" (Mt 16:16).

Peter was so astonished by his reply that he wondered if he had really spoken or if it had been someone else. He immediately thought of John. As if in a dream, he heard Jesus speaking to him, and there was no more doubt that he might be talking to someone else: "Blessed are you, Simon Bar-Jona! For flesh and blood has not revealed this to you, but my Father who is in heaven. And I tell you, you are Peter, and on this rock I will build my Church, and the gates of Hades shall not prevail against it" (Mt 16:17–18).

Yes, Peter heard these words as if he were dreaming, but every one of them was engraved on his heart, forever. His poverty, his misery were like a smooth stone inscribed with these words, through the power that came from Jesus alone. He did not understand these words at all, but he knew that they had been written inside him and that his entire life, his whole person, would have no form other than these words.

Silence followed. Jesus continued to look at Peter, and the other disciples did, too. Simon lowered his eyes like a timid child. He had never felt so small, so insignificant. When he looked up again, Jesus had already started walking again, and Peter felt happy to be following him.

6

"Get behind me, Satan!"

(Mark 8:33)

That was the first day on which Jesus began talking about his passion and death. This disturbed everyone. Of course, they could see that things were going badly between the Master and the authorities, and the situation was moving so fast that it wasn't far from being a matter of life and death. But what bothered them the most was that Jesus was proclaiming his death as if it were inevitable, like a destiny that nothing and no one could change. It was as if Jesus' mission could be realized only through the suffering and death that he was proclaiming and describing in a detailed manner. It was true that he was also talking about resurrection, but what could that mean? Jesus would certainly rise like all other just persons, because he was good and innocent; but he seemed to mean something different by the word "resurrection" than the Jews did.

The disciples talked about this with each other. What does this mean? Will he really die? And what about us?

So they all urged Peter—who seemed to have just received an important position from the Master—to find out from Jesus himself what their fate was to be.

Ever since Jesus had spoken those mysterious and solemn words to him, Peter had felt more important. Deep inside, he was trying to distract himself from his painful intuition of the real destiny that those words had foreshadowed. He perceived, in fact, with a sense of unease, that there was a connection between his new authority and what Jesus was saying about his own future of suffering and death.

So he found himself expressing some of these concerns, speaking to Jesus with an aggressiveness that he began to detest more and more as it emerged. Simon was defending himself, shielding himself from the unalterable destiny that was already uniting him to the Lord.

Jesus was used to Peter's personality. For his part, Peter was used to being corrected by Jesus, and he knew that he deserved it. But this time, the Master's reaction was so harsh that it took Peter's breath away. Jesus was not looking him in the eye as he always did: he was looking at the others. Did he know that his response also applied to them, who had sent Peter forward, or did he want to spare Peter from the flames of a look that would have burnt him to a crisp, while his words merely scalded him?

"Get behind me, Satan! For you are not on the side of God, but of men" (Mk 8:33).

Satan! Why this horrible name? Satan? The enemy of God! The one who destroys! So this is what Simon had become to his one true friend, the only one for whom he would give his life. Was it possible that Jesus did not understand that if Peter had spoken to him this way, it was because he loved him above all things and could not accept losing him, being separated from him?

He started to get choked up, and he would have wept if Jesus had not turned toward him. It was then that Peter saw in the Master's eyes an extreme weakness, and great anguish. He had never before seen fear in him, the human shadow of fear, an innocent fear like the kind that Simon had once seen in the eyes of a sick child past the point of crying any longer. Peter lowered his eyes: he was not worthy of looking God in the face.

7

"It is well that we are here"

(Mark 9:5)

Simon kept a low profile for the next six days: he stayed in the group and listened to Jesus, but he didn't dare speak, ask questions, or make his usual observations. Still, he could see that the Master's attitude toward him had not changed. Jesus didn't hold a grudge against anyone, not even against the Pharisees, with whom he argued so often. Jesus' anger was not like ordinary human anger. Peter was coming to understand that the Lord's anger was always the expression of deep suffering. Every time the Master was harsh or rough with them, they quickly understood that in that situation, Jesus had no other way to express how much he loved them.

It was true that the Master seemed to be more abrupt with Peter than he was with the others. At first, this had bothered Simon, because he had the impression that Jesus did not like him very much. But then he realized that the fault was with his own character. He was the one who provoked Jesus' reactions. Every time, Peter got irritated with himself:

"Do you always have to be making your observations, saying what you think, speaking out when no one has asked you to or when the matter doesn't concern you?" But every time, Peter was the first to ask for forgiveness, to make amends for his errors and his uncontrolled outbursts.

But with time, Peter realized that this explanation was too superficial, because he saw that Jesus never reacted instinctively. His patience was infinite. Peter understood that Jesus had nothing but love and desire for the other's good. He decided that he needed to think about what greater good Jesus might want for him, to treat him so harshly.

After his first reaction of wounded anguish, Peter began to reflect on Jesus' own reaction. The Master had never been so harsh and offensive with him, or with any other person. "Get behind me, Satan!" He had given him the title of his worst enemy, the one Jesus was fighting against. Together with the other disciples, Peter had seen many disputes between the Master and the demons possessing tormented people. And when he drove them out, it was horrible to hear the way they shrieked and shouted. Simon could not shake his sense of unease, a sense of fear that brought him one nightmare after another. He found peace only by drawing near Jesus, or at least by thinking about him.

And now, he was the one Jesus had called Satan! All because Peter rebelled at the thought that the Lord might suffer and die in a terrible manner. Peter wondered whether there was a connection between Jesus' prophecy that he would be the "rock" of his Church and his announcement of his own destiny. Simon would never, ever accept any position or honor at the expense of his Master's suffering and death. Never! Jesus should have understood this! Besides, what was the meaning of this talk about the Church and the Kingdom of God?

Peter fell silent. The Lord's violent reaction was making him understand that the connection between the mission entrusted to Peter and the death of Jesus was necessary and unbreakable. That meant he would never be able to reach the full depth of their friendship without embracing the Master's obscure destiny. Simon wondered if he had agreed to this as well on the day he had responded to the Lord's call with boundless joy. He thought back to the euphoric happiness of his first steps in following Jesus. Everything was so serene and simple. It was true that even back then there were a number of hardships to endure, but it was as if everything was immersed and covered over in the delightful experience of the rabbi's love and friendship. But now, the hardship was not something outside of this relationship, but inside it, and for Peter this was an unbearable affliction, because he no longer had any possibility of consolation outside of his friendship with the Lord. Yes, he really would be like Satan, lost, damned, far from God, if he no longer had this friendship, the only thing that had given him the certainty of salvation.

So Peter simply settled in to wait. He did not know what he was waiting for, but he understood that it was pointless to try to guess. It had to be something surpassing all the conjectures that were burning in his mind like a deadly fever. So he was relieved when, six days later, Jesus suddenly called him together with James and John to go to a secret place that not even the other nine disciples could know about. They left the villages behind and started climbing up a hill. They walked for several hours, amid a silence that the three disciples did not dare break, even to ask each other where they were going. Peter walked with a feeling of serenity in his heart. He imagined that something new was about to happen between the Master and him and that it would free him from the delirious thoughts that had been plaguing him for six days and nights.

Jesus was pensive, immersed in prayer. He walked in front of them, climbing the mountain along a rocky path at a steady pace that seemed intended not to disturb the depth of his thoughts.

When they arrived at the top of the mountain, Jesus began praying with the same gestures and mannerisms that the disciples saw in him often, although normally he liked to be alone when he prayed to the Father. But this time, Jesus did not try to withdraw from the three of them. So they began to feel increasingly uneasy about being so close to Jesus while he was praying, as if they were being forced to witness a secret that would become a burden on their consciences.

The people envied the disciples' intimacy with the great rabbi who attracted crowds and worked miracles. The disciples felt that this intimacy was becoming more and more profound, overcoming the weakness of their minds and hearts.

And ever since Jesus had begun to talk to them about the hour of his approaching suffering and death, he had become for the disciples like the burning bush for Moses: they were drawn to him, but the closer they got, the more they felt wounded by their own unworthiness.

These sentiments changed the relationships among the Twelve. The apparent gap between their lowliness and the mystery of the Lord united them in the desire for mutual compassion, although none of them could satisfy this. Peter felt increasingly close to the younger of Zebedee's sons, John. Jesus himself loved this disciple more than the others, but this preference did not bother them at all, because they intuited that it was something meant for all of them but that John had the virtue of accepting it in simplicity. This was why Peter sought out John's company more than that of the others. John and Peter didn't talk much, but John seemed to have a mysterious capacity to radiate to those around him the effects of his special relationship with the Master.

On the mountain, the three felt themselves driven to huddle together, to the same extent to which the distance between themselves and Jesus was growing larger. They stared at his face. Was he sad? Was he happy? It was as if in the Lord, suffering and joy were mysteriously brought together as a growing radiance gradually blinded their astonished eyes.

Waking and sleeping, light and darkness, sunshine and dark clouds, silence and deafening sound—all of this blended together before their eyes as they stared at Jesus. His face was familiar, but somehow it was now becoming unrecognizable.

Jesus was alone and silent, and yet there were two prophets conversing with him. The disciples could not hear anything of what they were saying, but they guessed that they were talking about what Jesus had been telling them for some time but they didn't want to hear. And it was as if the glorious light that was now blinding them was coming from those shadows the same way the golden sunrise emerges from the night.

Peter was surprised to find that he was happier than he had ever been before, and he also realized that the joy, like the light, had its source in the shadowy mysteries of which the three were speaking. Peter understood that he was participating in the joy of Jesus and that the sadness of recent days had no place there. How completely he felt Jesus' joy as his own! It belonged to him more than his sadness did. It was a joy that descended upon him, that rose up from within him; it came down from the sublime vision, reaching the misery he knew was his own, a misery that Jesus loved more than Peter could bear. He felt so loved the way he was, without deserving it, that it seemed completely natural to speak to Jesus in the midst of that light, as if it were just some everyday occurrence. He felt as if he could say anything, just as it came into his mind. He spoke like a child, saying just what was in his heart: "Master, it is well that we are here; let us make three booths, one for you and one for Moses and one for Elijah" (Lk 9:33).

But the dark shadow that suddenly fell over them froze the words on his lips, and his heart immediately lost the innocent childlike serenity that he thought he had regained just a moment before. "No, Simon, you are not innocent!" he was about to say to himself. Then another, more powerful voice silenced them all: "This is my beloved Son; listen to him" (Mk 9:7).

It was like a clap of thunder; but it was as if the

voice and the words had no beginning and no end. Although at that very moment everything around them
returned to normal, there was still an impression of
eternity on Jesus' face, terrifying and sweet at the
same time. Jesus looked at them and said peacefully,
"Let's go back down, but remain silent!"

8

"For me and for yourself"

(Matthew 17:27)

"This is my beloved Son; listen to him" (Mk 9:7). Peter concentrated on these words during the days that followed the experience on the mountain—not only because they had been so firmly imprinted in his mind but also because everything else about the incident had become hopelessly confused. It all seemed like a dream, or like a series of events that had happened too fast to keep track of them. The radiant transformation of Jesus, the presence of Moses and Elijah (how was it that he recognized them?), the words of the three about the Master's destiny, their sleepiness and their lucidity; Peter was unable to keep all of this straight in his memory, his mind, his emotions. He couldn't even talk about it with Jesus or any of the others.

But although the words that had echoed from the cloud had terrorized them, he now repeated them constantly, finding great serenity in them. At the time, they had driven away the almost childlike joy that had kept him at the surface of the event he was experiencing. But now these words brought him a consolation that no mother, no father could ever give a weeping child.

Jesus had often spoken of God as Father, as his Father. He had spoken to the disciples of his goodness, his forgiveness; he had told them that the Father thought of everyone with tenderness, just as he cared for the flowers of the field and the birds of the sky. But until the episode on the mountain, these things were something to believe in at the word of Jesus, not something they had experienced personally. They believed because of Jesus, because it was clear that he lived in this awareness. But feeling that they themselves were loved by God as by a good father was another question.

Now Peter, James, and John had heard the voice of this Father, and it had addressed them directly. Peter felt in his heart that, as severe as they were, those were truly the words of a Father full of tenderness.

"This is my beloved Son; listen to him." Peter thought back to another statement, the one he had found on his lips the day on which Jesus had asked them who he was to them. "You are the Christ, the Son of the living God" (Mt 16:16). Jesus had replied immediately, "Blessed are you, Simon Bar-Jona! For flesh and blood has not revealed this to you, but my Father who is in heaven" (Mt 16:17).

Jesus, Son of the living God, the beloved Son. Peter intuited that everything that was extraordinary about the Master, everything that was unique, all of his power and goodness, all his profound wisdom, everything, absolutely everything, had to come from the one reality defined by that title: Son of God, beloved Son of God.

"Listen to him!" the voice had said. Peter wondered if he really listened to Jesus. He had always listened the best he could, and "upon his word" he had accepted many things, many teachings that he was unable to understand. But now he thought back to those bitter words from the Master: "Get behind me, Satan!" Did he have to listen to this, too? Did he have to go away, leave the beloved Son of God who had just been revealed before their eyes upon the mountain? Could it be that the revelation of the tenderness of the Father had to coincide, for Peter, with obedience to Jesus, who was pushing him away, and therefore also away from the Father, whom Jesus himself was revealing to him?

His thoughts and feelings wavered between joy and dismay, until one day when an unusual episode gave Jesus the opportunity to make him realize that, in the eyes of the Father, there was nothing that separated them.

They had just come back from Capernaum, to Simon's house, where they usually stayed when they
were not on the road proclaiming the good news to
the people in the countryside. The tax collectors for
the temple came to Simon for payment of the custom-
ary tax. They also knew that the Master of Nazareth
often stayed with Simon, so they pointed that out
and made it clear that Jesus would also need to pay
the tax. Simon reassured them that there would be
no trouble, that Jesus would pay. In reality, Simon
had been intending to pay for Jesus as well, without
telling him. But Peter was not as prosperous as he had
been before, and as he went back into the house, he
wondered how he would be able to honor his debt.

As soon as he had entered the house and his eyes
had become accustomed to the dimness, Simon saw
Jesus looking at him, and before he could say a word,
Jesus smiled and asked him a strange question: "From
whom do kings of the earth take toll or tribute? From
their sons or from others?" Peter answered that it is
the subjects, not the sons, who pay taxes to the king.
"Then the sons are free", Jesus observed. He continued, "However, not to give offense to them, go
to the sea and cast a hook and take the first fish that
comes up, and when you open its mouth you will
find a shekel."

For a moment, Peter thought that if anyone else
had said this, it would have been some sort of trick to

mock his naïveté. But then Jesus said something that changed everything. "Take that"—there was something like a glint of mischief in Jesus' eyes, "and give it to them for me and for yourself" (Mt 17:27).

It was not the prescience of Jesus, nor the little miracle of the coin in the fish's mouth (which Peter was sure would come true even before he went to the sea)—it was the last words of Jesus that went right to Peter's heart, carrying him up where joy is so great that it is hard to distinguish from suffering.

Only Jesus could understand what he was feeling, and, before Peter burst out sobbing—which the others might have seen as hysteria—Jesus sent him back outside; "Go! Do it quickly!" The sea alone witnessed the tears and the laughter of the apostle who had been forgiven but who above all was reinforced in his certainty that he shared, together with Jesus, the condition of beloved son of the Father.

Peter took the coin, released the fish back into the water, and sat down on the sand, where the calm waves marked the rhythm of his first real prayer to the Father of Jesus, and his Father.

9

"How many times must I forgive?"

(Matthew 18:21)

How beautiful the lake was at sunset!

After the strongest wave of emotion had passed, Peter savored the sweetness still inside him, like the light, cool breeze of the lake that refreshes the fishermen after their day's work.

He was forgiven! For the first time, he understood that he was forgiven! Simon quickly reviewed in his mind the miraculous catch of fish that had unsettled him the first time Jesus had climbed aboard his boat. He could hear himself shouting again, "Depart from me, for I am a sinful man, O Lord" (Lk 5:8). Now he truly understood that in that moment he had not understood what he was saying. He hadn't yet known what it meant to be a sinner, or to be forgiven. Now he could no longer say to Jesus, "Depart from me", because the true sin he had committed had been that of separating himself from him. He had withdrawn from him by judging him, presuming that Jesus would adapt to his thoughts instead of adapting his own thoughts to those of Jesus. He had judged Jesus! Could this be the sin of Satan?

"Listen to him!" the voice of the Father had thundered. Yes, Simon had not listened to the Lord; his heart did not want to listen to him anymore while he was speaking of his suffering and death. Peter believed that he was reacting this way out of love, but in reality he was following his pride. He believed that he knew better than Jesus or the Father what was good and what was evil. What could he, Peter, know about the plans of God?

And when he felt condemned, lost, and rejected, couldn't that have been his pride controlling him? He was declaring that Jesus could no longer forgive him, and this was even worse than the first sin, because it put a limit on the love of Christ—his own limitation. Yet Jesus had immediately shown the same friendship, the same attention, the same kindness as always. But Peter wasn't listening anymore; he wasn't paying attention. His thoughts were a clamor of resentment drowning out everything that love is able to express only in silence.

He had not understood the immense love that Jesus had shown by choosing him to climb Mount Tabor. He had not understood the infinite love of the Father in splitting open the heavens in order to speak to him: to him, Simon, the poor, prideful sinner!

"For me and for yourself". These words had shattered his thoughts, his judgments, his point of view, leaving nothing in him but a bare heart, poor and wounded but aware that it was a treasure in the hands of the Father. Peter understood that the mercy of the Most High he sang about in the psalms and the other prayers at the synagogue meant that God stooped down to eliminate the unbridgeable, infinite distance between them. It was forgiveness, and only forgiveness, that had saved him and set him free.

Forgiveness. But what did it really mean to forgive?

Simon began reflecting on his life, on his relationships with others. Forgiving. Jesus spoke about it often, and when he did he almost always used the example of the Father, who is good both to the good and to the evil.

Forgiving. Could it be that he, too, had to forgive? It was true that Peter absolutely could not stand certain people. He had argued with many others about work or about family matters. Now he had to admit that he did not really love all of the disciples who followed Jesus. He even detested some of them. For example, he never could stand Judas, mostly because of his ambition. How could the Master tolerate having someone like that around? Others he just didn't like. He recognized their abilities and the progress they were making, but he avoided them as much as he could because of their character, their way of acting

and being, and their manners. Matthew the tax collector, for example, had left all of his money behind
in order to follow Jesus, and at that moment Simon
had sincerely admired the immediacy of his response,
without any ifs or buts. The trouble was that in his
judgment, although Matthew had left his money behind, he had not gotten rid of his habits as a publican,
a tax collector, and even a bit of a parasite. It wasn't
Matthew's fault that he had never been taught to do
anything but count the money that others earned by
the sweat of their brow, but Peter was a coarse working man; he couldn't stand those kinds of people!

The women around Jesus also bothered him. Some
of them were too excitable; others were from wealthy
families, and Peter felt like riffraff around them. If it
hadn't been for the Lord, he would never have associated with people like that! But then Peter had another
thought, and laughed to himself—the others would
never have associated with someone like him either!

In other words, there were people to forgive and
opportunities to forgive every day, at almost every
moment. Did he really have to do this? And how?

He realized that up until then, he had listened to
Jesus' teachings about forgiveness with only half an
ear, as if they didn't really concern him. But now that
he had gone to the limit of the desire for forgiveness
and of the joy of being forgiven, the question of forgiveness was beginning to burn inside of him, and he
understood that he would not be able to preserve the

joy of the forgiveness he had received without being willing to listen to Jesus' teaching about the practice of forgiveness.

Peter got up and went back into the house. Night had already fallen, and they told him that the Master had gone out to pray by himself, as he usually did. Peter did not see him again until the following day, and since all of the other disciples were there too, he tried to pose his dilemma in the form of a rabbinical question: "Lord, how often shall my brother sin against me, and I forgive him? As many as seven times?" (Mt 18:21).

Jesus could not conceal a little smile, accompanied by an expression of compassion. Only Peter noticed it, and already he was starting to blush because his question was too theoretical and had nothing to do with his experience the day before, or with his usual way of talking with Jesus.

Jesus seemed to play along, and with a touch of irony he echoed the rabbinical style of the question, giving Simon an arithmetical formula that was too much for him: "I do not say to you seven times, but seventy times seven" (Mt 18:22).

But as soon as he saw Peter's brow furrow at the complicated multiplication, he translated it into a parable with exaggerated contrasts, better suited to engaging the minds and imaginations of his disciples. He told them about a king who forgave an immense debt for his servant, who was unable to pay him. But just after this, the same man had another servant jailed because he owed him a tiny sum. The king had the first servant punished harshly and told him, "Should not you have had mercy on your fellow servant, as I had mercy on you?" (Mt 18:33).

Peter lowered his eyes pensively, but he felt the eyes of Jesus penetrating him as he delivered the moral of the parable, stressing each word: "So also my heavenly Father will do to every one of you, if you do not forgive your brother from your heart" (Mt 18:35).

A great silence fell among them. They had all taken on the same expression as Peter, and for a long time the shadow of sadness on Jesus' face had nowhere to fall except upon the coals in the fireplace, until finally John looked up at him, his eyes full of the humble repentance of the innocent.

10

"Lord, to whom shall we go?"

(John 6:68)

The crowds looking for Jesus became larger and larger. For the disciples, it become more and more of a strain to stay with the Master. This was especially true when they stayed in the city—they had no peace, day or night. Peter was happy only when he could be alone with Jesus, on the deserted roads in the countryside, or even better, on a boat on the lake. Often, when they were leaving an inhabited area, they had to depart in the middle of the night—but even then, the cries of the poor and the sick echoed behind them for a long time, giving them the unpleasant feeling that they were doing something wrong.

All the people, all the poor were a bit annoying, but at least they were seeking Jesus with love, or at least with desire, and listened to him. It was clear that to them, the rabbi was their last hope for a happier life.

Peter had never experienced so much misery as he did in following Jesus. The sick, the insane, the possessed, the lame, the blind, the deaf-mutes, and even a number of lepers were coming to be healed and consoled by the Lord. All of these people depleted the Master's energy, but Jesus never showed any annoyance at their presence. If he had to leave them to go to another city or region, he knew how to do this with sensitivity, without making them feel rejected or abandoned. Their encounter with him left them all with the impression of a friendship that would last forever.

No, it was not the poor who really wore Jesus out, but another category of people who approached him: those who were hostile to him, always waiting for the slightest word or action that might confirm their opposition to his teaching and work and justify a condemnation.

Like flies, they emerged wherever Jesus went. Some of the rabbi's teachings seemed to get through to them, and some of his good deeds seemed to stir their hearts—but no miracle was able to convince them. They were able to twist any word of truth and turn any experience of life into dry wood to feed the fire of their misrepresentation, as if there were no room inside them anymore for anything but lies.

Jesus, who was always so merciful toward human misery, knew how to use the strongest possible images and representations to describe their twisted spirits. His friends and disciples understood that for him, the greatest threat was that they, his followers, might become hypocrites, like the scribes and the Pharisees. Peter clearly saw that the hypocrisy of the Master's enemies consisted in a prideful self-centeredness that was capable of exploiting even his truth and goodness for the sake of the lust for power. So when Jesus found even the slightest trace of this hypocrisy in his disciples, he was very severe with them—but they had come to admit that beneath this severity was an even greater love for them.

With the passing of time, these two movements—of the crowd seeking him and of the Pharisees threatening him—became more intense. The disciples were pulled between these two forces, until the day on which, after multiplying the loaves and fishes for the second time, Jesus gave an incomprehensible discourse in the synagogue of Capernaum. He compared himself to the true bread that had come down from heaven, a bread given by the Father. Then he said something even more puzzling. He said that without eating this bread, no one could have eternal life, and that the bread was his flesh, that one must eat his flesh and drink his blood in order to have life and be saved. He said that he, Jesus, would raise up on the last day those who believed in him, because he was the life of the world.

These words made Peter's head spin, and he was both fearful and angry about the effect they would have on the crowd, especially on the Jews who were hostile to the rabbi. And in fact, Simon could see on the faces of the people that their astonishment, disgust, scandal, and hatred were growing.

Jesus spoke gently, and the contrast with the evident hostility of his audience made him look like an innocent lamb surrounded by wolves. The dissatisfaction and complaining increased, but he seemed not to notice. Instead, he repeated the things that the people did not want to hear, like a child who becomes more indiscreet because he doesn't understand how nasty grown-ups can be.

The Twelve huddled together. Were they with Jesus? Were they with the scandalized crowd? The fear and bitterness of disappointment took hold of their hearts. It was hard for them to see the Master's reputation being ruined by a few words that were obscure and above all imprudent. When Jesus finished speaking, with his expression even more luminous than after speaking about the Father, the apostles realized that even those following Jesus as disciples would not hesitate to leave him, scandalized.

Jesus became sad because they did not believe, they did not yet believe that he had been sent by the Father. They had followed him because of what he said and did, not for who he was. For them, a discourse they could not understand was a reason to leave him, more decisive than who he was for them, more decisive than all the love that they had experienced in his presence. How could they not understand that his presence was the bread that nourished them and gave them the fullness of life, a life as the beloved children of the Father?

Many of them left, forever.

The Twelve stayed. They didn't dare move a muscle or speak a single word. There seemed to be a heavy silence emanating from the heart of the Lord and spreading around him like winter fog. Can there be any sadness greater than that of the rejection of a gift, at the very moment when its full value is displayed?

But although the people's ability to receive seemed to have been exhausted, the Lord's gift of love could never be. The suffering on his face betrayed a tranquil decision to make an offering of himself that could penetrate this rejection of him and express the "folly" of a love that wanted to save everyone.

Gently—but as if a boundary were near that could be crossed with a single word—Jesus looked at the little group of confused apostles. "Will you also go away?" Peter was surprised for a moment when he recognized in the Master's voice the same tone that he had heard one day from a boy with leprosy, asking them for alms from the side of a country road. An immense sadness took hold of him, and the only reply he could manage was a cry for help. His cry, too, was like that of a beggar: "Lord, to whom shall we go? You have the words of eternal life" (Jn 6:68).

II

"You shall never wash my feet!"

(John 13:8)

It was from that moment that the Jewish authorities decided to try to have Jesus put to death. This was partly because the crowds continued to seek him out and admire him and partly because they realized that the number of his faithful disciples had diminished. Moreover, after those discourses on the bread of life, it had become easier to condemn him as a blasphemer or to depict him as a madman.

It was also from that moment that Jesus added another detail to the announcements on his passion and death: he revealed that one of them, one of the Twelve, would betray him. Once, he even said, "One of you is a devil" (Jn 6:70).

All of the apostles were deeply distressed by this and did not dare talk about it, neither among themselves nor with Jesus. For Simon in particular, these words were like a slap in the face, reminding him of the day on which the Master called him "Satan". Was he the "devil" who would betray the Lord? He could never do such a thing, never! He found himself examining the others, one by one, to detect the future traitor. He would watch him to prevent him from carrying out his betrayal, even if he had to kill him with his own hands.

But these thoughts did not free him from his sense of unease or from the nagging fear that he might in fact be the one who would commit the detestable crime. How many times, in fact, had he said or done something he had sworn to avoid at all costs!

Jesus didn't give them any help in figuring out who the traitor was, because he remained just as friendly with each of them as before, and even seemed to favor and prefer the ones Peter looked at with the most suspicion.

All of this did not foster harmony among them. There seemed to be a malevolent spirit haunting the little group, turning the slightest problem into an opening for the veiled hostility that was poisoning all of them. It was as if they no longer felt like brothers but like rivals in a competition for a position of power that the Master would assign to one of them. But if they looked at Jesus, the image he projected was certainly not one of power but of a weakness that seemed pushed to an extreme already visible in his eyes.

Without really acknowledging it to themselves, the Twelve began to avoid his gaze, because it unmasked a betrayal lurking within all of them.

The feast of Passover was approaching. Since they had begun following him, the disciples had celebrated this feast with the rabbi. This year as well, Jesus would tell two of them to go prepare everything necessary for the Passover supper. He sent Peter and John into the city, where a man carrying a jar of water would bring them to a house where they could all eat the Passover meal in one large room.

Peter was happy for the opportunity to get away from the group of the Twelve for a while and also for the chance to spend some time alone with John. In contrast with his typically youthful cheerfulness, John was quiet and withdrawn. Peter watched him out of the corner of his eye as they walked rapidly toward the city. All of a sudden, he realized how much even John had changed. Three years before, when they were fishing together, he had been little more than a boy. Now he seemed to have become a man, with a maturity like that of Jesus, more in the expression than in the physique.

John noticed that Peter was looking at him, and responded with a bittersweet smile. Peter then realized that the similarity between Jesus and this young man lay entirely in the luminous depths of their eyes.

They arrived in the city. Everything was abuzz with preparations for the feast. Peter started getting nervous, because he couldn't see the man with the jar in the teeming crowd. He started muttering, and John

told him, in a quiet voice but with a strange authority that made Simon blush, "Hold on, stay calm. You
know that everything will happen just as the Master
told us!"

In fact, just a few moments later they saw the man
with the jar, and then there was nothing else to do
but confirm that everything was nice and ready.

That evening, Jesus arrived together with the ten
others.

Each one took his place in silence. Peter understood that the silence that had accompanied the group
along the entire journey was like a natural projection
of the sadness of Jesus himself.

Everything was ready for the start of the ritual
prayers and the meal. But as soon as everyone had sat
down, Jesus stood up. It was not the host's job to get
up if something was missing, so the Twelve moved
to get ready to take care of whatever it was that had
made the Master stand up.

Astonished, they saw him take off his tunic, wrap
himself in a towel, pick up a basin and fill it with
water, and then start going around the table washing their feet and drying them with the towel. Jesus
did this with an unusual sense of concentration. His
actions were slow and deliberate. He showed great
attentiveness in washing the dust from their feet, and
the same care in drying them.

At first the Twelve were almost frozen as they stared at him, and then they began nervously looking at each other. No one knew how to react, how to interpret all this. And since they couldn't understand it, they just let it happen. Everyone was waiting for someone else to react, without having the courage to take the initiative.

Simon felt the tacit pressure from the others being focused on him as Jesus gradually approached him. They knew that Peter always reacted, and that evening, any reaction from Simon, even an outburst, would be like a summer storm lifting the heavy atmosphere of silence and tension.

Jesus was already kneeling in front of Peter and was about to put one of his feet into the basin. Simon could express his refusal only by instinctively pulling back, which immediately seemed ridiculous and childish to him, and when he spoke even his voice sounded like that of a petulant child: "You shall never wash my feet" (Jn 13:8).

Peter was expecting a tough response from Jesus—maybe he even wanted this, because severe corrections had always been the Lord's way of showing that he loved him. But the face of the Master, kneeling at his feet, had the same expression of sadness and calm that it had shown since the start of this Passover supper. Jesus' extreme gentleness accentuated the contrast

with Peter's erratic behavior. "What I am doing you
do not know now, but afterward you will understand.
If I do not wash you, you have no part in me" (Jn
13:7–8).

Peter was not used to letting himself be treated deli-
cately. The people loved him because he had a good
heart, but they seemed to adapt themselves to his
character by showing their affection for him in his
own coarse, headstrong way. Even Jesus had treated
him this way—until now. But not that night. The
Master's expression, his words, his servile posture
—it was all like the breeze of the prophet Elijah, a
breeze that emanated from a gentleness that seemed
to be drawing everyone toward a mysterious and secret place, like the Holy of Holies in the temple of
Jerusalem.

Peter realized that he had never washed the Lord's
feet; he had never thought he would have to do so.
He had always respected the customs: servants and
women were the ones who did this sort of thing.
Peter had never washed anyone's feet. Now it was
too late. And he understood that it was too late. The
Master had wanted to wash his feet, not the other way
around. Jesus didn't need Peter to wash his feet. It
was Peter who needed this. Suddenly he was seized by
the same sense of unworthiness that he had felt after
the miraculous catch of fish, when he had shouted,

"Depart from me, for I am a sinful man, O Lord" (Lk 5:8). But that was after he had seen the power of the rabbi, after he had seen an astonishing miracle. Now, instead, Jesus was nothing more than a servant, like the least of the servants. What was this meekness, this humility, supposed to mean? Peter understood that this was the way Jesus was, that this was who he was, that in the three years they had spent together, Jesus had never been anything other than this: a humble servant at the feet of the people, and of his own disciples.

Over the past three years, Simon had focused his attention on the Messiah's power, his majesty, his glory, that glory which was punctually confirmed by miracles, making that glory ever more desirable, as the drunkard thirsts for wine.

Peter had always wondered why Jesus did not exploit his powers more, why he always hid after his miracles, why he always asked his disciples to remain silent and not talk about them.

Peter did not understand the reason, but with a hint of terror he intuited that this was who Jesus was. It was as if he had come to the brink of a precipice. Until now, he had always felt that he was moving toward a destiny of power and victory; for him, following Jesus was like climbing a mountain—he knew that sooner or later, they would come to the peak. The experience on Mount Tabor had confirmed this sense of euphoria. Suddenly Peter understood that the destiny Jesus was offering him was not a pinnacle of victory but an abyss of humble love, its depth unfathomable. He felt an enormous desire to cast himself into this abyss, with everything he had: "Lord, not my feet only but also my hands and my head!" (Jn 13:9).

He did not understand Jesus' answer, but it really did seem that he was plunging into Him, dirty and weary like his feet, that he was plunging into that mysterious ocean whose breadth and depth could be seen in the sad expression of Jesus.

12

"I will lay down my life for you"

(John 13:37)

Jesus went to put the basin and the towel back in one corner of the room. He put his tunic back on and returned to his place. No one dared say anything or ask him any questions; everyone was staring at the table, at the food, at the dishes. Only John was looking at the Master, waiting for what he would do or say next. From following Jesus, he had learned that it was important to look at him: by observing him, he could grasp the meaning of many things, even if he didn't always understand them. It was John more than anyone else who had understood that the important thing was to love Jesus, that loving him was the best way—no, the only way—to understand him. But he had also learned that in order to love the Lord, one must accept suffering, suffering along with him. After all, how is it possible to love someone without sharing that person's sufferings?

John had truly followed Jesus; he had followed him in silence, with his heart. It was as if he had followed the Master where he was going, not only with his footsteps, but with his heart, his decisions, his teaching, his works.

Peter, on the other hand, couldn't bear to look at Jesus that evening. He was too afraid of his suffering; he was afraid of following him like John.

Peter instinctively looked at John, as he often did; he watched him looking at Jesus. But he immediately lowered his eyes, as if he were violating a sacred mystery of friendship.

It did not take long for Jesus to break the silence. He spoke to them of mutual service. But Simon was unable to pay attention, because these words did not seem to have the same impact as the gesture of the washing of the feet and the warning that the Master had given to him shortly before: "If I do not wash you, you have no part in me" (Jn 13:8).

By now, there was only one thing that Peter feared: being separated from Jesus. This fear had haunted him constantly over the past three years, and the wound of those words, "Get behind me, Satan!" had never completely healed. Peter was afraid of the pain he would suffer if this wound were reopened. This was why he tried to control his instinctive words and reactions. He wouldn't be able to bear it if the Master ever said anything like that again.

Peter regretted his opposition to Jesus' gesture. It seemed that he had run the risk of being rejected by Jesus. He had been quick to ask the Lord to wash his hands and head as well, but he wasn't sure that he had made up for his stupidity.

And what did that mean, that statement Jesus had made at the end: "You are clean, but not all of you" (Jn 13:10)? Could he be the unclean one? What did it mean to be clean or unclean?

Peter was jarred out of these thoughts when he heard Jesus say, in a voice trembling with a sudden onset of anguish: "Truly, truly, I say to you, one of you will betray me" (Jn 13:21).

It was not the first time that the Master had told them this. But he had never said it with such anguish before.

The Twelve looked at each other. Peter realized that what was bothering him the most was not the fact that there was a traitor in their midst, and not even the possibility that it might be him, but the sudden realization that Jesus was in anguish, that Jesus himself was afraid.

He wanted to reassure the Master and defend him from the danger that he feared. He was determined to find out, once and for all, who was threatening to betray Jesus.

John was sitting between him and Jesus. Peter whispered to him, "Ask him who he's talking about." John nodded. Peter saw him lean over to Jesus. He could guess what their brief conversation was about, even though he couldn't hear anything. But instead of telling him what Jesus had said, John leaned back on his cushion again, looking intently at Jesus.

Simon didn't dare distract him, so he also watched Jesus, who took a morsel of bread, dipped it into the dish, and gave it to Judas. He took it nervously, awkwardly, and gulped it down right away. He couldn't meet Jesus' eyes. Then Jesus said something to him, and Judas left without saying good-bye to anyone, as if he was in a hurry to leave the city, already enveloped in night.

Strangely, as soon as Judas had closed the door behind him, it was as if everyone could feel that the oppressive atmosphere had been lifted. It didn't become more joyful, but more intimate. The sadness and anguish could find shelter among them, in the friendship that united all of them to the Lord. Only at that moment did Peter understand that Judas was the traitor. But he had no time to lash out in anger against him, because Jesus immediately began speaking to them in a tone of calm authority. He talked about the Father, and about the Spirit who would console them; he talked about love and friendship, and about the sadness that would be turned into joy; he talked about the unity between him and the Father, and about the unity among them.

Peter let these words penetrate his heart without worrying about understanding them or even remembering them. He knew that they were true, because Jesus was speaking them. They were not separate from the Master: they were his Word, they were he himself. The only thing he had to worry about was staying close to Jesus. Jesus would make sure that he understood what he needed to understand, that he remembered what he needed to remember.

Then, together with his words, Jesus added a gesture that seemed like the rituals of the Passover supper of the Jews, but there was something different about it, a different meaning. He took bread, blessed it, broke it, and gave it to them, saying: "Take this, all of you, and eat it; this is my body." Then he took the cup of wine and, giving it to them, said, "This is my blood of the new covenant, which will be shed for many for the remission of sins."

The apostles were hesitant as they passed the bread and drank the wine. They ate and drank because Jesus wanted them to. Peter looked for a moment at the red wine in the cup that he was raising to his lips. "My blood shed", he thought as he drank it, almost against his own will. Did drinking it mean that he accepted that Jesus would shed his own blood? Never! He would never agree to this! He would do whatever he could to prevent it! He was certain of that!

As if he were reading his mind, Jesus began to tell them that all of them would abandon him that very same evening, that they would all be overcome by their fears and run away, leaving him alone. He spoke calmly, without any hint of criticism in his voice. Instead, he seemed to be deeply moved somehow. He wasn't looking at anyone in particular; it was as if he were talking to himself, his eyes fixed on the platter in the middle of the table, the only evidence of the lamb that had just been completely consumed.

But Simon felt that these words were addressed to him, like a response to his thoughts—as if Jesus had struck up the conversation with him alone. He exclaimed vehemently, "I will never give in! I will never disown you! I am ready to go with you, for you, to prison and to death!" But the vehemence of his words was like a powerful wave that breaks against the rocks, dissolving into foam. And the rock was the Lord's sad and meek expression, sunk into a solitude that no one could presume to console. Peter heard himself say again—no more than a moan this time —"I will lay down my life for you."

"Will you lay down your life for me? . . ." Jesus began to reply. It seemed that he didn't want to finish the thought—and Peter would have preferred that, because Jesus was looking at him the way he always did when he wanted to penetrate the inmost depths of his stubborn heart. "Truly, truly, I say to you, the cock will not crow, till you have denied me three times" (Jn 13:38).

As if to leave no time for a pointless and humiliating reply, or out of pity for Peter's embarrassment, Jesus stood up and asked everyone to leave with him.

They followed him without comment, without questions. The night air was cool, the streets were empty, but they felt at ease as soon as they left the city and came to the garden past the Kidron Valley, so familiar to them. Entering the garden, one thought stabbed into Peter's heart: "Judas knows this garden, too!" But he didn't have time to think about it, or about the angry fear that came with it. Jesus was calling his name, and calling for James and John also, telling the others to stay where they were. He gestured to the three to follow him. Peter thought about the experience on Tabor. Would Jesus be transformed before them again? What a comfort that would be on such a dark and sorrowful night! But as soon as Jesus— walking in front of them amid the olive trees, their trunks twisted by the ravages of centuries—turned toward them, Simon saw in the torchlight an expression of anguish that drove away any illusion.

After saying, "My soul is very sorrowful, even to death; remain here, and watch with me" (Mt 26:38),

Jesus withdrew into the night. The flickering torchlight occasionally lit up his form, kneeling there. In
the total silence of that hour, his voice reached them
distinctly. But they were little more than sighs and
groans. Peter could only make out words like "Abba",
"cup", "your will". Jesus was repeating them insis-
tently, persistently.

Left alone without Jesus, the three looked at each
other in confusion. "Watch with me", he had told
them. What did that mean, watch with him? What did
it mean to join him in a prayer in which he showed
he was lost and abandoned?

During the last three years, they had more or less
learned to pray with him, to pray when he prayed. It
was enough to remain in silence, repeating some frag-
ments of a psalm or the prayer to the Father that Jesus
had taught them. They had understood that praying
with Jesus was like entering into his prayer, participating in his prayer. This all seemed to have become
easy to them. Yes, this calmed them and brought back
their serenity of heart, which they often lost in the
midst of the noisy and oppressive crowd.

But this didn't make sense anymore. How could
they pray with Jesus, how could they enter into his
prayer if Jesus was no longer their solid and steady
support, if Jesus' prayer was itself all about fear, if
Jesus no longer seemed united with the Father, if
Jesus even seemed to be fighting with the Father?

The three suddenly realized how much their inner stability depended on the Master, how dependent they were on what took place between Jesus and God, his Father. Why in the world had Jesus dragged them into his trusting relationship with the Father if now this relationship seemed to be deteriorating and leading to death?

Peter looked at John, as if looking for support in this abyss into which they were all falling, together with the Master. But John's eyes were like a close-up reflection of Jesus' anguish.

It was getting cold, and the torch was going out. Simon sat down, thrust the torch into the dry ground, and wrapped himself in his mantle. The others did the same. They fell into a sleep burdened with sadness, but without nightmares. The nightmare was all around them.

How much time went by? They awoke to the voice of Jesus. He was standing there next to them, but there wasn't enough light to put an expression to that sorrowful voice. He asked them to watch, to resist sleep and temptation. Then he withdrew again.

Peter shook himself awake and knelt down. "Do not enter into temptation": what did these words of Jesus mean? That night, everything was so absurd that words no longer corresponded to any concrete reality.

Peter tried to stay awake, but everything was so empty inside of him and all around him. He no longer thought of anything. He no longer loved anything. He no longer suffered . . .

He realized that he had fallen asleep only when Jesus came a second time and addressed him directly: "Simon, are you asleep? Could you not watch one hour?" (Mk 14:37). But he didn't wait for a reply. Peter wanted to be near Jesus and help him, but he felt that Jesus was drawing further and further away, toward an inaccessible place. Simon felt like a father powerless beside his incurable, slowly dying child. He wasn't really sleepy, and James and John weren't either: sleep was their only defense in the face of a sadness so great it was beyond their capacity to bear.

When Jesus awoke them the third time, the torch had gone out for good, but the Master's form could be seen clearly in the moonlight shining through the olive branches. Peter could tell immediately that Jesus was not the same as before. His voice was firm, determined: "Are you still sleeping and taking your rest? Behold, the hour is at hand, and the Son of man is betrayed into the hands of sinners. Rise, let us be going; see, my betrayer is at hand" (Mt 26:45–46).

It was no longer the complaint of a man in distress: these were the words of a general determined to fight. What had happened while they were sleeping? What kind of strength had he been given? But when Peter stood up, he found himself face-to-face with the Lord, and in the moonlight he could see that his skin was covered with a dark film. He instinctively lifted a hand to touch one of his cheeks, but at that very moment they heard a group of soldiers coming, and the next thing they knew they were surrounded by men holding torches and lanterns.

Peter recognized Judas in the front of the armed group and saw him coming forward quickly to kiss the Master: the lantern he was carrying lit up Jesus' face again, and Simon saw that the film on his skin was blood. He couldn't tell what Judas and Jesus were saying to each other. All he could catch was the Master whispering, "Friend".

When he heard this, Peter realized that the Lord had been betrayed. Until that moment, he had not really understood what betraying Jesus could mean. He guessed that one could only betray a friend and that only someone who loved as much as Jesus did could really be betrayed. And only one of his friends could really betray him.

Simon was overwhelmed by an uncontrollable rage: he unsheathed the sword he had brought and hurled himself against the men surrounding the Master, determined to kill Judas first. But the darkness of the night and of his hatred kept him from striking cleanly. All he could do was wound one of the guards' ears before he was pinned by the others.

Jesus was calm. He was in control of everything that happened next. He reprimanded Simon for his violence. Then he healed the guard's ear. "Shall I not drink the chalice which the Father has given me?" (Jn 18:11). And he said to the guards, "If you seek me, let these men go" (Jn 18:8).

The Master's calmness unsettled everyone: both the guards, who had been prepared by Judas for a difficult and violent arrest, as well as the disciples, who were expecting Jesus to ask them for help. It was as if it had been the Master, and not his enemies, who had decided on and orchestrated the arrest.

The disciples were overpowered by the fear that Jesus seemed to have placed in his Father's heart. They all ran away while Jesus, watching them, calmly held out his hands for the ropes that would bind him.

13

"I do not know the man"

(Matthew 26:72)

They started running in all directions. They were afraid of staying with Jesus, afraid of the group of soldiers, afraid of Judas, afraid of remaining together, of being recognized together as disciples of the Master. They were afraid of their own fear and were disgusted with themselves, so most of them ran a long way, aimlessly, as if to lose themselves, to escape their thoughts and their wretchedness. Running is often a false substitute for courage, a final squandering of vital energy before plunging into defeat. Human pride would rather suffer violence than confess its own weakness.

They all dispersed, except for Peter and John. By an unexpressed instinct of friendship, the two ran off together—but they were as aimless as the rest, their flight being an end in itself.

They came to a halt in the open countryside. Simon stopped because he was out of breath. John stopped to stay with Simon but also because his thoughts had turned back toward Jesus, reviving his love. They fell to the ground at the foot of an olive tree.

For a long time, the only sound was their gasping for breath. Then Simon alone was panting. Then there was quiet, and the two lay there for a moment as their heartbeats settled down.

"Simon." John said it feebly, but it was enough to startle Peter.

"Simon", he said again, since Peter hadn't said anything. "We have to go back to Jerusalem!"

Simon didn't react, as if to put off answering. He couldn't say anything but yes.

John stood up. "Are you coming?"

Simon answered almost angrily, "Of course, I promised!"

"Promised? What did you promise? To whom?"

"I promised Jesus that I would defend him, that I would die for him, and I haven't forgotten!"

John didn't say anything. They started walking, guessing the direction based on what they knew about the area and trying to retrace their chaotic steps. They finally reached a road. It was empty, and they started walking down it accompanied by their dark thoughts.

"Where would they take him?" Peter wondered out loud.

"It had to be the residence of the high priest, or of the procurator . . ." John answered.

"They won't let us in."

"I know someone close to the high priest. I'll see if I can get us inside."

"And after that? What will we do? We're alone, with no weapons . . ."

"We'll see . . ."

They walked in silence. Simon could feel that his fear was still there. But he continued to repeat his promises to Jesus: "I will not deny you! I am ready to go with you to prison and to death! I will give my life for you . . ." But the more he repeated his oaths, the less courage he felt to keep them. He made up his mind all the same and prepared to sacrifice himself for Jesus. His first attempt had come to nothing—in part because of the darkness—but now he would do everything he could to follow through.

He looked at John. In the early morning light, he could see that the features of his face were drawn. But it wasn't just fatigue. Peter realized that John was praying.

The city streets were still mostly empty. At the door of the high priest, John asked to see the person he knew there. They looked at him with suspicion, but they let him in, and Peter with him.

John was allowed into the building. Peter had to stay out in the courtyard.

A group of guards and servants had lit a fire and were warming themselves, waiting for something else to happen with the supposed Messiah they had handed over to the priests. Peter wanted to stay away from them, even though it was cold. But he realized that he would be more conspicuous off by himself. And since the rest of them were all wrapped up in their cloaks, he figured it would be fairly easy to blend in with them. He sat down behind them, drawing part of his cloak over his head and face. The men didn't notice him, but the servant woman who had opened the door came toward the group with an expression that was both curious and confident. After seeing Peter with John, she had started thinking about where she had seen them before. She had finally placed Peter's face among those of the friends of that rabbi of Nazareth everyone was talking about, the same one she had seen pass in front of her the night before, bound and escorted as if he were a bandit.

She approached the formless heap of cloth that Simon had become, pointed at him, and exclaimed triumphantly, "You also were with Jesus the Galilean" (Mt 26:69). Everyone heard her—that was her plan —and fell silent, turning to look at the little of Simon's face that could be seen in the light of the flames. "I don't know what you're talking about", Peter growled dismissively. What was this meddling about? He didn't have to answer to anyone, let alone a gossipy servant woman and these vulgar soldiers.

He left the group and began walking around the courtyard, making it clear that he wasn't trying to get away, he just didn't enjoy their company.

Since her revelation hadn't made much of an impression among the guards, the servant went to one of her fellow servants, certain that she could get a better reaction. The other servant woman went over to Peter and stared at him with no hesitation and then shouted to her friend and to the guards, "This man was with Jesus of Nazareth" (Mt 26:71).

Seeing that everyone was beginning to recognize him, Peter shouted, "I do not know the man" (Mt 26:72). This time, he was more fearful than dismissive.

But now the men had been swayed by the women's interest in this stranger. They approached him, surrounded him, and asked the guards who had been present at Jesus' arrest what they thought. "He has a Galilean accent!" "He's the one who cut Malchus' ear!" "Yes, he was definitely in the garden with the rabbi!"

Peter felt like he was done for. He trembled as each man came up close to inspect him, pointing an accusing finger at him. Desperately, he screamed and swore: "I'm not one of his followers! I don't know what you're talking about! I don't know that man!"

The guards were about to arrest him, but at that very moment the dignitaries and guards came out with Jesus tied up in their midst; so when he shrieked his last denial, Peter wasn't looking at the harsh and menacing faces of the guards. He was looking right at Jesus, who was looking back at him. There was enough daylight that Peter could see every nuance of the Lord's expression.

For a moment—but how long is a moment before the gaze of the Eternal?—everything around Peter disappeared. The guards, the servant women, the courtyard, the residence of the high priest, the fire, the chill . . . everything vanished. There was nothing but the Lord's face—and in it, Peter saw again everything he had lived through with the Master: the lake, the boat, the first catch. He could hear all of the Lord's words, and his own words to him: "Put out into the deep"; "But upon your word"; "Depart from me, for I am a sinful man, O Lord"; "Henceforth you will be catching men"; "You shall be called Cephas"; "Bid me come to you on the water"; "Lord, save me!"; "You are the Christ, the Son of the living God"; "Blessed are you, Simon . . ."; "Get behind me, Satan!"; "It is well that we are here"; "For me and for yourself"; "How many times must I forgive?"; "Lord, to whom shall we go?"; "You shall never wash my feet"; "I will lay down my life for you"; "Remain here, and watch with me"; "Simon, are you asleep? Could you not watch one hour?"; "Put your sword into its sheath; shall I not drink the chalice which the Father has given me?"; "The cock will not crow, till you have denied me three times" . . .

But all of these words, all of these events were, in Jesus' eyes, nothing other than a story of love, and for the first time Peter understood, even saw, how much Jesus loved him, how great a friend he was. The words of his denial—"I do not know the man" —were reflected in the Master's eyes, so full of love and suffering, and fell back into Peter's heart like salt on a wound. He had never truly loved the love of Jesus, and he measured within his own heart all of the solitude, all of the abandonment of his only Friend and Father. No, it was not the Jews, it was not the Romans who wounded Jesus that night, but him, Peter! The abandonment of friends is a wound more painful than the hostility of enemies.

Now Peter really would have given his life for the Lord. Now he understood that he was willing to lose everything for him. And in that endless instant —which will never end—Simon asked Jesus, with his eyes, if he could die for him. And in that endless instant, the Lord answered with his eyes, Not now! Later! And in that endless instant, Peter did not object; he accepted the gift of powerlessness, the gift of being unable to do anything, the gift of the failure of his will, the grace of the powerlessness of his love. Simon, called Peter, accepted the wound of seeing Jesus with no one to love him and felt the bitterness well up inside of him.

The cock crowed.

Jesus was gone.

Peter was already outside, shedding the blood of his tears for Jesus.

14

"They both ran"

(John 20:4)

It was dawn on the first day of the week. For Peter, it was the first time he had been awakened since Jesus had stirred him in the garden of Gethsemane. Peter had not really been able to sleep since that night. He hadn't slept in the past few hours either—it was more as if his body had given in to the exhaustion of his spirit. For two days, after the denial in the courtyard of the high priest, after the cock had crowed, he had been left alone—more alone than ever before. Now he truly realized how rich his life had been with Jesus. It wasn't that he was dying without him—that would have been a relief—but he had nothing to think about except his own nothingness. He had become the witness of his nothingness. He was nothing but the bitter awareness of having no more substance or foundation. He was nothing but this awareness, condemned to be nothing but this, forever, because nothingness cannot change itself and cannot extinguish its awareness of itself. So he could not sleep anymore, but he couldn't stay awake either, because staying awake implies a relationship with reality, and for Peter there

was no more reality, now that Jesus wasn't there anymore. He wasn't there because Peter had denied him;
he had denied having anything to do with him: he
had denied a bond like that of a child in his mother's
womb, that allowed him to exist.

Devoid of substance, Peter was no longer afraid either. Fear implies that there's something there to be
threatened. But there was nothing left in him, nothing to fear any threat.

So after wandering aimlessly all day on Friday, he
was not afraid of going back to the house where the
disciples had eaten their last meal with the Master.
He didn't really decide to go back there—out of in-
ertia, out of habit, he had been brought by the sunset
back to the city, and the streets of the city led him to
this house. He wasn't looking for anything in particular, and he wasn't expecting to find anyone he knew.
Could he still find a familiar face, could he still meet
anyone, now that he could no longer encounter the
Lord Jesus?

For that whole day, the world no longer existed
for him. There were dark clouds in the noonday sky,
and there was an earthquake a few hours later, but if
nothing is real, what can these upheavals mean?

He knocked at the door. A servant woman opened
it, recognized him, and stood there looking at him.

It was obvious that she had been crying. Peter didn't say anything—but why should his conscience be so disturbed by a simple servant woman who opens a door?

He went to the top floor. In a corner of the room, which was still as he had last seen it—for a moment, he looked at the empty cup—he saw a little group of people whom he recognized: the owners of the house, a few of the women of the group, John— there he was; where had that coward been hiding?— and at the center of the group, like its heart, tiny and wrapped up in her mantle, the Mother of Jesus.

Mary saw Peter and went toward him, leaving the others sitting in the corner of the room. Peter did not dare look her in the face. She put her hand on his arm, squeezing it feebly. "You're here, Peter?" she said, without expression, in a voice heavy with suffering. "Come sit; you're tired." But Peter didn't follow her back to the group. He sat down in the opposite corner and hung his head down between his knees. For a moment, Mary's voice had reminded him that he existed, but it was an existence in which he felt the absence of Jesus and his own nothingness even more keenly.

John and the women were looking at him. John stood up to go toward him, but Mary held him back and he sat back down next to her, in a silence broken only by the sobbing of Mary Magdalen.

Peter could never explain afterward what had happened during those two days. How can there be memory where time is no longer? And how can time exist if there is no more relationship? And how can there be a relationship if there is not another to say "you"?

On the morning of the first day of the week, Simon woke up to the rustling noise of the women leaving the house with jars of aromatic oils to go to the tomb—this is what they were saying to each other —to anoint the body of Jesus. It was still dark, and Peter closed his eyes, but he couldn't fall asleep again.

Go to the tomb? What tomb? Peter realized that he hadn't yet thought that if Jesus was dead, his body had to be somewhere.

His body. Was there something left to testify that the Master had been a reality? Was there something of him that could still be touched? He was jealous of the women who would soon be able to touch the precious body of the Lord, see his face again, even if it was lifeless, and touch his hands. But how would they roll away the stone that must be blocking the opening to the tomb? They needed a man to help with that, and to lift the body. "I should have gone with them", Peter said to himself. "Why didn't they ask me? And why didn't John go with them? And Mary —why doesn't she show any interest in this care for the body of her Son?"

He made a decision, the first in two days. Did he still have a will? He got up and got ready to go to the tomb of Jesus. But at the door, he suddenly realized that he did not know where they had buried him. He hesitated for a moment. He turned toward John and Mary, who were praying together, sitting at the table where Jesus had broken the bread. "Where is the tomb of Jesus?" he said, surprised at the sound of his own voice. Mary and John interrupted the murmuring sound of their prayers and looked at him in bewilderment. John said sadly, "It is in the garden near Calvary, where he was crucified."

Crucified! The word struck Peter as though it were an arrow through his heart. He approached the two of them as if he were recognizing them for the first time. Quietly, he repeated, "Crucified? Did you see it?" Mary hid her face in her pallid hands. John nodded, his teary eyes looking at Peter with pain.

"Did he . . . did he . . . did he suffer much?" But he saw the Mother of Jesus put her hands to her chest, one clenched in a fist, the other pressing her heart, as if to stop a hemorrhage. But before John could answer, Mary turned her eyes toward Peter— eyes that suffering had made deep and pure as the Sea of Galilee—and said, in a voice that was weak but resolute, "Peter, remember that he said he would rise again!" Simon and John lowered their incredulous eyes so that Mary couldn't see them.

"I'm going to the tomb", Peter said again, already walking toward the door. Then there was the sound of hurried steps on the wooden staircase. The door was flung open, and there stood Mary Magdalen. Breathlessly, she cried out, "They have taken the Lord out of the tomb, and we do not know where they have laid him" (Jn 20:2).

John seemed to read something in her eyes, like she was trying to tell them, "Go and see!" He got up and left, followed by Simon.

They ran without thinking about the weariness that had built up over the past three days. Peter was following John, who was running faster and knew the way. He remembered their flight after what had happened at Gethsemane, when they had returned to the city. But why were they running now? Was it because they wanted to reach a tomb from which the body of Jesus had been taken, the last remnant of a physical reality that could provide them with at least a memory of their friendship with the Master?

Peter ran faster, trying to drive these thoughts away. But why was his heart so full of eagerness?

When he arrived, breathless, at the garden, he saw John already bent down at the opening of the tomb, trying to peer inside in spite of the pitch darkness. John let Peter enter first. Why? Was he afraid? Simon asked himself. But in the look that they exchanged, he realized that John was granting him the primacy that he himself had betrayed for the past three days.

They entered the tomb. Peter waited for his eyes to adjust to the darkness. His heart was racing. He didn't dare to stretch out his hand to touch anything. He was afraid that his unspoken hope might be confronted with a cold corpse. Gradually, his eyes began to make out the shape of a white shroud, long enough for a man, lying on a stone. It was empty. The body wasn't there. The tomb was empty. John was looking over his shoulder. Peter turned to him, and his questioning eyes met the face of an astonished child, breathless, surprised by a joy that surpassed the ability of the eyes, the voice, the hands to express it. Peter started to say, "Do you actually think that . . ." But he understood that John would not be able to say any better in words what his entire being was already saying.

They left, both gripped by the urgent desire to go back to the Mother of Jesus and tell her. Tell her what? They did not know, and they knew. But as soon as they walked in the door, they could tell by her eyes that Mary already knew everything.

15

"Simon, son of John, do you love me?"

(John 21:15)

For forty days, they lived in the euphoria of knowing that at any moment the Lord Jesus could appear, and they could touch him, listen to his voice. Time lost all meaning for them, because there was no other point of reference than these appearances of the Risen One, more important than the rising and setting of the sun, more real than day and night, than sleeping and waking, than food and work. More important, and yet these appearances gave everything an intensity that they had never experienced before. Everything crackled with the anticipation of his appearance, everything was in a state of waiting for Jesus, any situation in life could suddenly become the place and circumstance in which he chose to manifest himself. He met them in closed rooms, on country roads. Sometimes they did not recognize him at first: they mistook him for a farmer or a pilgrim, a common stranger, and then suddenly their eyes would be opened and they would recognize him, their hearts exploding with joy.

Sometimes he didn't say anything; other times he explained the Scriptures. He even reprimanded them because at first many doubted that he had truly risen, that it was really he who had appeared, in flesh and blood, and not just a spirit.

Now they knew that he had truly risen; they could no longer deny the evidence. But no one could predict when he would appear—he alone decided when and how he wanted to manifest himself. In this way he was educating their desire, their expectation, and their attention. Now any pilgrim they met on the road could be him. Any stranger, any poor beggar might all of a sudden display the beloved face of the Lord. Any moment, even the most ordinary, could become the moment of his presence.

Jesus appeared while they were praying but also while they were working or intent on carrying out the most ordinary duties of everyday life.

All of this conferred an extraordinary intensity on their lives. Even relationships among them changed. Sometimes Jesus appeared to all of them together, sometimes to one or the other of them. Then they would tell about these encounters, and their testimonies filled everyone with joy because everything that Jesus said or did for one was for all.

They grew interested in learning everything about his suffering and death because Jesus explained the Scriptures to them, demonstrating that all of this had been announced by the prophets and in the psalms. They even remembered all of the words that he had said to them during the years when they were with him. Together they listened to the stories of John and of the women who had climbed Mount Calvary. They made them tell them over and over again about everything that Jesus had suffered, the words he had spoken, and the moment of his death.

It was Jesus himself who prompted them to do this, because when he appeared to them he often showed them his hands and feet with the wounds still in them from the nails, and a large wound in his side, the one that John had seen a Roman soldier inflict with a spear after Jesus' death.

Mary was silent; she preferred to let John and the other women speak. Since the morning of the Resurrection, she had radiated a tremendous joy, but it was as if this joy had not driven out the suffering from her. For her, it was like joy and suffering went together, as if the risen life of Jesus had not erased the marks of his death on the cross. Mary was in their midst like a silent flame of love, too bright and too intense for them to approach without fear, like when Moses came to the burning bush. And yet the Mother of Jesus maintained her absolute simplicity among them and continued to serve them humbly, being attentive to each one. Nothing that they felt in their hearts escaped her; she was not indifferent to any of their joys or sufferings. And even when she did not speak, it was evident that the flame of her prayer embraced everything in a boundless trust in Christ the Lord.

John never left her after this. Jesus had entrusted them to each other, and it was if they had nothing more to do than live out this last wish of the crucified Lord. But for the others as well, their communion had become something like a new home to which they could always return, to revive the flame of the love of Jesus. It was as if the risen Jesus was always present between Mary and John, always simply there.

Peter sought them out; he needed their presence, their companionship. He needed to be in silence with them, close to their mystery. Mary and John did not conceal their own affection for Peter and showed him profound respect. Every time a decision had to be made, they asked for his advice, and if there was disagreement among the disciples, they said they agreed with Peter, that Peter had to decide, that Peter was right. This bothered him, because he had not forgotten his misery, but he understood that they were doing this out of love for the will of the Lord. He understood that he, too, had to obey the mystery that had penetrated him, even if it was a source of suffering to have to live out this vocation with the awareness that he no longer deserved anything and was the last of all.

His suffering over having denied Jesus would not go away. The Resurrection had filled him with an indescribable joy, but it had not eliminated his repentance. Instead, it had made this more intense. Every time he saw the Risen One, it was as if the joy entered his heart through the wound of his denial. Every time he saw Jesus' body still wounded by the nails and the spear, and when he was talking about Jesus' sufferings, it was as if Judas, the priests, the Roman soldiers, all of those who had hurt Jesus, were identified with him and him alone. He, and no one else, had handed Jesus over; he had accepted that he should be abandoned, mistreated, and crucified and that he should die.

Jesus seemed to have nothing in particular to say to Peter. Peter wanted to speak with the Lord about his denial; he would have preferred for Jesus to reprimand him; he wanted to throw himself at his feet and ask him for forgiveness and a severe penance. The Risen One had chastised all of them for their lack of faith in the testimony of the women who said he was alive. Strangely, he did not criticize their cowardice in fleeing and abandoning him during the passion. And Peter thought that what he had done in the courtyard of the high priest was more serious than not having believed the excited testimony of a few women.

Nonetheless, Peter accepted this sorrowful joy. Maybe this was a penance that the Lord would inflict on him for the rest of his life. He also got used to thinking that the Lord had justly revoked the primacy that he had promised to him one day on the shore of the lake. This was another reason why the behavior of Mary and John made him uncomfortable. Others, like James, one of Jesus' relatives, seemed more suited to take responsibility for the group. Peter also loved the idea of being able to love Jesus in simplicity, in poverty, in the shadow of his luminous presence.

They soon left Jerusalem and returned to Galilee. It was a great relief to be able to abandon the city where they had suffered so much. Galilee greeted them with all the serenity of its spring season—the olive trees, the green grass, the fragrances in the air, and the blue of their beloved Sea of Tiberias, on the shore of which they had experienced so many happy moments with Jesus. They stayed in Capernaum, in the houses of Simeon, the sons of Zebedee, and other friends.

They went back to their usual activities almost immediately, always with the freedom that they found in their attachment to no one but Jesus, their friend who had conquered death.

One evening, Peter felt the need to go back out onto the lake. "I'm going fishing", he said to those who were with him, without thinking that everyone would join him. The night fell gently on the tranquil water. Peter pushed the boat out onto the lake, rowed out, and cast the net—and then realized that he was doing this not because he wanted to fish but because he wanted Jesus. One day he had encountered the Master while casting his nets; he had encountered him in accepting to row back out onto the lake; he had encountered him on this same boat, doing the things he was doing now. He now realized that he could do nothing, experience nothing without desiring that Jesus be present with him, in their midst.

At the first light of dawn, they decided to go back. Simon was disappointed not because they hadn't caught anything but because Jesus had not appeared.

A stranger approached them on the sandy shore and called out to them from a distance, "Children, have you any fish?" (Jn 21:5). They answered bluntly, almost in unison, "No" (Jn 21:6).

They looked at one another in amazement. John stared intently at the stranger. They cast their nets, without even paying attention to what they were doing. Immediately the nets were full. John whispered to Peter, "It is the Lord!"

Peter recoiled. Of course! Who else could it be? How could he not have recognized him at once?

Without thinking, Peter jumped into the water, to the astonishment of his companions, except for John, who understood everything.

Jesus was smiling at him. They looked at each other, but Peter did not dare speak. There was already a fire there near Jesus, with a fish roasting on it, and some bread. The fire seemed to have been burning for a long time. As soon as the others had reached them, Jesus turned to them, saying: "Bring some of the fish that you have just caught" (Jn 21:10). Simon did not leave the others any time to react: he jumped onto the boat and, with an immense effort, dragged the net to the shore by himself. Jesus continued to smile and, without waiting any longer, said, "Come and have breakfast", giving each of them pieces of roasted fish and bread.

Everything was so simple, so natural, just like it used to be—and yet the man who was standing in front of them, looking at them, serving them, touching their fingers with his own, and eating with them, smiling silently, was the one who had been crucified and had died!

How wonderful it was to be there with him as the sun rose, turning into gold the countless waves on the lake that seemed to bolster the joy within their hearts.

Jesus waited until everyone had finished eating. It seemed that this experience would never come to an end. Ah, if only it had never ended!

But suddenly the Lord, who until that moment seemed to have been paying equal attention to each of them, looked closely at Peter. Simon could not stand this gaze for long because it was identical to the one that he had seen in the courtyard of the high priest. He looked down at the fire, but the fire also reminded him of the courtyard, the guards, the servant women, himself. He closed his eyes and listened to the waves caressing the pebbles on the shore. He had the impression that the voice speaking to him was also a wave from the deepest abyss: "Simon, son of John, do you love me more than these?" (Jn 21:15).

Peter had long stopped expecting Jesus to speak to him personally, and if he expected anything, it was a reprimand or correction. He would never have imagined that the Risen One would simply ask him if he loved him. He had prepared to respond to a severe correction; he had prepared to ask for mercy, weeping, admitting that he was a sinner, vile, the last of all . . .

"Do you love me?" and again, "more than these", "more than these", meaning more than John, who had followed him all the way to the foot of the cross?

But what struck Simon was not only the Lord's question but the tone in which he asked it. Jesus was not testing him; this was not a trial. Jesus was begging for his love, begging for what he needed.

Peter was there, in the midst of his companions, but now everything was taking place between himself and Jesus, as it did in the courtyard of the high priest.

Simon was alone before Jesus, who was in need of his love. He didn't need a sword to free him from the guard who was holding him or from the Jews or the Romans who wanted to take his life. Jesus needed love, his love.

"Yes, Lord; you know that I love you."

Jesus added, not as a question, but as a simple statement: "Feed my lambs."

There was silence. Peter could have started talking about something else, anything else, just to extend the pleasure of being there together. But Jesus continued to look at Peter, and Peter did not lower his eyes, because he had just told Jesus that he loved him, and because Jesus, with his thirst for love, could not be feared.

Peter heard his name spoken a second time, and he recoiled again. "Simon, son of John, do you love me?" (Jn 21:16).

Had he not said the right thing? Or had he not been sincere? Didn't Jesus believe that he loved him? Peter repeated the question to himself: Do I really love him? But what does it mean to love Jesus? How can I pretend to love him? How can I believe that Jesus needs my love?

He looked into the Lord's eyes. It was as if the Lord's expression was giving the right shape to the raw material of what he wanted to say. Peter repeated, "Yes, Lord, you know that I love you." And once again, in the same tone, Jesus said to him, "Tend my sheep."

Jesus looked out toward the open lake, and Peter did the same. The sun had already risen, and the rippling water sparkled under its warm light. Peter was admiring the view when he heard Jesus say his name again and, turning quickly, saw that he was already looking at him. "Simon, son of John, do you love me?" (Jn 21:17).

This time, Peter found an explanation for this threefold repetition of the question: I denied him three times, so he asks me three times if I love him. Does he not believe me? Can I still say anything about myself or about Jesus after I swore three times that I didn't know him? But if he does not believe me, if he cannot believe me anymore, why tell me to feed his flock?

With tears in his eyes, with a voice like that of a child who is about to break out sobbing, Simon said so loudly that he almost scared himself, "Lord, you know everything; you know that I love you!"

And once again, once and for all, before he had even finished answering, Peter saw with certainty that Jesus believed in his love, that he had believed in this from the first answer, that he had always believed it, since their first encounter on this same shore. Only now, only at this moment, after living with him for three years, after seeing him suffer and after he had died following Peter's denial and abandonment, only now was Peter discovering that Jesus needed his love, that Jesus, the Son of God who had conquered death, was thirsty for his love.

"Feed my sheep", Jesus repeated, and Peter understood that this task was connected to the question that the Lord had asked him. Peter had only one mission left in life: that of loving Jesus Christ, of responding to his thirst for love, and of responding to this as the sinner that he was, as miserable as he was. It was as if Jesus was telling him, "You can deny me a thousand times, you can deny me your whole life, but never forget to love me, never deprive me of your love!"

A gentle breeze started blowing the scent of the lake toward them. The coals in the fire Jesus had lit began glowing again. The other disciples were happy, as if Jesus had spoken with each one of them. Jesus lightly touched Simon's arm and said, "Follow me!" But all Peter could hear was, "Do you love me?"

Epilogue: The Shadow of Simon Peter

From the day on which, after Jesus ascended to heaven, the Holy Spirit descended upon them in the upper room, their lives had changed completely, even more than when they followed Jesus through the streets of Palestine. They no longer had a moment for themselves: from sunrise to sunset, it was as if they were suspended between the mercy of Christ and human misery. But now the mercy of Jesus was no longer something that they observed from the outside, like when they used to watch and listen to the Lord. Now the mercy of the Lord was in them, like a fire, like a powerful wind propelling them toward the immense misery of the crowds. Peter thought back about what Jesus often said when he looked at the crowds that came to him: they were like lost sheep, without a shepherd, and his eyes were sad and fiery at the same time. He suffered because of all of this misery, but he burned with the joy of being able to give them himself, the meaning of their lives, their everything.

Peter and the others now felt the same sentiment of sadness mixed with ardor. This was why they did not tire of feeding the flock, of starting over each day to proclaim Jesus Christ as the only salvation of the world.

Peter thought back often to the image that Jesus had used to describe himself during the last supper before the passion: "I am the vine, you are the branches. He who abides in me, and I in him, he it is that bears much fruit, for apart from me you can do nothing" (Jn 15:5). How true that was! Without him, nothing; with him, everything! Simon seemed always to be living at the limit of his capabilities, and even beyond them. He spoke to the people, but he didn't know what to say; he healed the sick, but he knew that this was impossible for him; he corrected, but he knew that he deserved to be corrected by all. Everyone asked him for time, words, actions, miracles, attention, and love, and he knew that he had none of this in himself: he always felt like he was empty, exhausted, at the limit. The Lord had cast him into an adventure he would never be able to master.

Before encountering Jesus, Simon could keep his entire life under control. Home, family, fishing—it was easy to keep his little world under control. He was obeyed at home, he was a good fisherman— and in spite of everything, the lake was generous— and the hired hands respected him. But now everything had become unmanageable. Hundreds, thousands of people of every race and language came to ask him for the impossible. The community of disciples continued to grow, and he was responsible for it. There was no more day and night, no regular meals, no time to snooze on the shore of the lake. And yet he felt calm, at peace. He felt inside himself a strength that did not at all eliminate his weakness, but used it.

Everyone was asking him for everything, and Peter responded to everything and to everyone. But he also responded by asking for everything from the Lord Jesus, who gave him his Spirit, the Spirit of the Father.

Ever since Jesus had begged for his love—"Do you love me?"—Peter lived by begging for his own, begging for everything from him. For this reason, the immense demands of the mission that Jesus had entrusted to him was not a burden. Everything was embraced in the exchange of love with the Lord, and it was a delight to hear himself called by the Lord in the voice of the poor, the sinners, all of these people in distress. It was a gift to be able to answer the Lord over and over again: "You know that I love you!" in every word he spoke, every action he performed, every step he took.

He no longer said, "I will lay down my life for you!" He simply said, "Take me!"

One of the things that the Risen One had said on that morning of light kept coming back to his heart: "When you are old, you will stretch out your hands, and another will fasten your belt for you and carry you where you do not wish to go" (Jn 21:18).

Thinking back to Gethsemane, Peter remembered that Jesus had also been bound and taken where he did not want to go. And yet how greatly he desired to go where the Father was sending him, even to death on the cross! Yes, now every day Peter felt the joy of being able to love Jesus by allowing himself to be carried, by everyone and by everything, where he would not have wanted to go except for Jesus. Yes, it was joy and the height of freedom to sacrifice one's own will for the will of the Beloved. What freedom, to want what would be undesirable except for love!

"You will stretch out your hands, and another will fasten your belt for you and carry you where you do not wish to go."

Stretching out his hands, empty hands, in order to permit himself to be taken wherever the Lord wanted —this was everything, his entire task. Jesus was asking him for nothing more. For this reason, Peter loved to spend a long time in prayer, as soon as he could, stretching out his empty hands toward heaven, toward the Lord. But he was no longer able to isolate prayer from the rest of his life: his hands were always stretched out, always empty, always ready to let himself be taken and led by Christ in everything, by Christ in everyone, always.

One day, walking along a crowded street in Jerusalem, in the midst of people shoving each other to see him, to listen to him and ask him for healing, Peter realized that the miracles took place even if nothing but his shadow passed over the sick (cf. Acts 5:15). This gave him a strange sensation, different from the instinctive impatience that he felt toward the crowd when he realized that they were more excited about him than about the Lord, who was the one who did everything. Was his shadow really enough to work God's wonders? He paused for a moment, looking at his shadow on the dusty and grimy road. The sun was high and distorted his shadow, with the head scrunched too close to the body and the arms stretched down to the feet. He looked up to check how high the sun was in the sky, but it dazzled him and he had to close his eyes immediately. When he looked back down at his shadow, it had a ghost image of the sun at its center, as if his own outline in front of him had a heart of fire that blazed over everything, even the grubby street and the beggars pressing to ask him for mercy.

He remembered something that Jesus had said there, in Jerusalem, during the Feast of Booths: "I am the light of the world" (Jn 8:12). Yes, only Jesus was the light, only Christ was the sun of life, of his life and the life of all the people. And yet it was not the sun that had healed these sick people, but its shadow. Without the sun there would not be the shadow, but without the shadow there would not be the healings. What a mystery! That the Light of Christ would act in a shadow! Peter looked at his shadow again; he looked at it fondly, as if he were looking at a child. He looked at it with gratitude: So you're the one who proclaims the light of Christ in me? You're the one who shows the world that the Lord is its light? You're the one who acts like the sun, warming, illuminating, healing, and making every living thing grow and bear fruit?

He thought back to the many shadows in his life: his character, his stubbornness, the words and actions he regretted, the things he had failed to do. Above all, he thought about the three years he had spent living with Jesus: what a waste of opportunities, what a lack of attention and docility! And he had been living with the Light of the world, with the Lord of the universe! And like always he thought about his betrayal, so slimy, so stupid, so stingy. Shadows, shadows, shadows everywhere, always shadows. Everything in him was shadows! And yet it was his own shadow that healed and saved all of these people. It was his shadow that was light and life for all of these people in need! Christ was using his shadow to manifest his divine Light to the world!

An idea broke through his thoughts and made him turn back suddenly toward the sun. The sun never sees the shadows! The sun manifests our opacity, but it does this by illuminating us, and the shadow that it creates is never in its view. Once again Simon thought about the expression of Jesus. Jesus had never looked at him to expose his misery, not even in the courtyard of the high priest. The expression of Jesus always illuminated—it illuminated everyone, even Judas, even those who crucified and insulted him. Only we sinners see the shadows on other people's faces, because there is no light in our eyes. Oh, of course Jesus knew our opacity, but his heart could not help but love it, forgive it, redeem it, save it, purify it with the light of his eyes.

Another sick man, prostrate on the ground, stood up rejoicing, healed by Peter's shadow. He began running, praising God. Peter did not move; he looked at the ground where the sick man had been lying. Now his shadow was even shorter, and the head had disappeared into the trunk, as if it had plunged into the heart. "Don't think you're great", Simon Peter said to it; "you're good only because the Lord looks with love on my misery!"

He continued on his way with a light heart, because his opaque humanity was now entirely the sign and instrument of the mercy of Christ.